THE SECRET WORLD OF THE ZEN BUDDHIST MONK

D.T. SUZUKI

ILLUSTRATIONS BY ZENCHU SATO
INTRODUCTION BY MORGAN BUCHANAN

FLOATING WORLD

ABOUT FLOATING WORLD PRESS

Japanese woodblock prints from the Edo period are termed *ukiyo-e* — images of the floating world. The term *ukiyo* is also an ironic allusion to the homophone *ukiyo* ("Sorrowful World"), the earthly plane of death and rebirth from which Buddhists sought release. Floating World press is dedicated to publishing unusual, interesting and enlightening content- that promotes a cultural harmony between East and West. Our books seek to embody a traditional aesthetic of form and function—beautiful words, beautiful design.

This edition Copyright © 2025 Floating World Press
Introduction Copyright © 2018 Morgan Buchanan

All rights reserved. No part of this book may be used or reproduced in any manner whatsoever without written permission except in the case of brief quotations embodied in a critical article or review.

First published in Kyoto by the Eastern Buddhist Society, 1934
First Floating World Edition 2018
Originally published as The Training of the Zen Buddhist Monk

10 9 8 7 6 5 4 3 2 1

ISBN: 978-17636021-0-6

Cover and interior design by Aspect Moon
Sanskrit proofreading Rev. Dr. John Dupuche

ORDERING INFORMATION: Floating World books are available online, through chain and independent bookstores worldwide or via direct order at www.floatingworldpress.com. Special discounts for bulk orders are available. Email contact@floatingworldpress.com

CONTENTS

INTRODUCTION..................................i

PREFACE...v

PART ONE
INITIATION......................................1

PART TWO
LIFE OF HUMILITY.............................21

PART THREE
LIFE OF LABOR................................31

PART FOUR
LIFE OF SERVICE..............................43

PART FIVE
LIFE OF PRAYER & GRATITUDE...............69

PART SIX
LIFE OF MEDITATION..........................87

APPENDICES & GLOSSARY..................141

INTRODUCTION

KWATZ! **I THOUGHT I'D** start with the sudden cry a Zen master makes to startle his student into enlightenment just in case it triggered, in you the reader, instant Zen. Then there's no need to read the rest of this book, but at the same time you won't complain about having bought it if the first word alone enlightens you.

If the sudden *kwatz!* failed to have the desired effect, not to worry, read on.

In our daily life, the weight of societal expectation grows more burdensome with time. We recognise there's something wrong with our relationship to reality. As we travel the road of adulthood, in the direction that our responsibilities demand, we have the feeling of moving further and further away from something invisible and essential. The further we progress from that invisible source, the more unbearable life becomes.

What is that thing we are moving away from?
What is the thing that suffers?

If you have this experience but no solution then, like the monk entering the Zen Buddhist monastery, you might have to undergo some training, some preparation to break down the wall that has formed between you and the living universe.

But life is too busy and you have far too many demands to enter a monastery and seek enlightenment. Not to worry, you have wisely invested in this book.

The Secret World of the Zen Buddhist Monk can be read in two ways—as a description of what happens to the Zen monk from his arrival at the monastery as a pilgrim to the daily rhythm of life he encounters there. Or it can be read another way—as if you are the monk—as if his tradition is your tradition, his process, your process.

I mentioned above that the monk's life is one of rhythm but it's not a pleasant rhythm, no easy escape. In fact as a monk you find that life is now an intensified version of the 9 to 5 of modern work life—unbreakable routine, unbreakable rules, strict discipline. Your new life hasn't removed the weight of society, instead it has focused and increased it until you are at a psychological breaking point. And then, with an inescapable mountain pressing down on you, a radical element is thrown into the mix—a thing that is absent of the duality encountered in every aspect of material existence, the wrecking ball of "I"—the Zen koan.

The koan is strange, paradoxical in nature—what is the sound of one hand clapping? If a tree falls in the forest and no one is there to hear it does it make a sound? What was your face before you were born? These have become Western clichés and as such it's tempting to drift past them and not look deeper. But try to see the koan with new eyes, the prajñā eye, that gives direct insight into the true nature of things. The koan has the ability to turn the mind back on itself and trigger instant Zen, an immediate awakening.

Here's one I tell my students—what state is the light globe in when it is neither "on" nor "off"? Still no enlightenment? Maybe you need to come at it more slowly. In that case, let this book be your koan. As you read, let Suzuki-sensei's account tune you. Read the surface level of the book but absorb the inference. What is it that the rules of the monastery and the behaviour of the monks refer to? They all point to something, but what is the "something" that is not said?

At worst this book will be like rain falling on dry earth, it will soften the ground and prepare you for a change of consciousness, start tuning you into the Zen frequency.

At best, the book as koan, will trigger an awakening. That's the thing about enlightenment, you don't know when it will hit. External noise will become distant, the internal chatter of the mind will vanish, there's only a feeling of space, lightness, stillness. You see things clearly as if looking down from a great height. The experience might come after you've put this book down, or when you're washing the dishes, or crossing the road—things might suddenly align, awareness might seep to the surface and dissolve the self or it might strike suddenly and shatter the self, like lightening, or the falling stick of a Zen master—*KWATZ!*

MORGAN BUCHANAN
Melbourne, May, 2018

PREFACE

FOR THOSE WHO have not read my previous works on Zen Buddhism[1] it may be necessary to say a few words about what Zen is.

Zen (ch'an in Chinese) is the Japanese word for Sanskrit dhyāna, which is usually translated in English by such terms as "meditation," "contemplation," "tranquillisation," "concentration of mind," etc. Buddhism offers for its followers a triple form of discipline: Śīla (morality), Dhyāna (meditation), and Prajñā (intuitive knowledge). Of these, the Dhyāna achieved a special development in China when Buddhism passed through the crucible of Chinese psychology. As the result, we can say that Zen has become practically the Chinese modus operandi of Buddhism, especially for the intelligentsia. The philosophy of Zen is, of course, that of Buddhism, especially of the Prajñāpāramita[2] highly coloured with the mysticism of the Avatamsaka.[3] As Zen is a discipline and not a philosophy, it directly deals with life; and this is where Zen has developed its most characteristic features. It may be described as a form of mysticism, but the way it handles its experience is altogether unique. Hence the special designation "Zen Buddhism."

The beginning of Zen in China is traditionally ascribed to the coming of Bodhidharma (Bodai Daruma) from Southern India in the year 520. It took, however, about one hundred and fifty years before Zen was acclimatised as the product of the Chinese genius; for it was about the time of Hu-nêng (Yenō)[4] and his followers that what is now known as Zen took definite shape to be distinguished from the Indian type of Buddhist mysticism. What are then the specific features of Zen, which have gradually emerged in the history of Buddhist thought in China?

Zen means, as I have said, Dhyāna, but in the course of its development in China it has come to identify itself more with Prajñā (hannya) than with Dhyāna (zenjō). Prajñā is intuitive knowledge as well as intuitive power itself. The power grows out of Dhyāna, but Dhyāna in itself does not constitute Prajñā, and what Zen aims to realise is Prajñā and not Dhyāna. Zen tells us to grasp the truth of Śūnyatā, Absolute Emptiness, and this without the mediacy of the intellect or logic. It is to be done by intuition or immediate perception. Hui-nêng and Shên-hui (Jinne)[5] emphasised this aspect of Zen, calling it the "abrupt teaching" in contrast to the "gradual teaching" which emphasises Dhyāna rather than Prajñā. Zen, therefore, practically means the living of the Prajñāpāramitā.

The teaching of the Prajñāpāramitā is no other than the doctrine of Śūnyatā, and this is to be briefly explained. Śūnyatā which is here translated "emptiness" does not mean nothingness or vacuity or contentlessness. It has an absolute sense and refuses to be expressed in terms of relativity and of formal logic. It is expressible only in terms of contradiction. It cannot be grasped by means of concepts. The only way to understand it is to experience it in oneself. In this respect, therefore, the term Śūnyatā belongs more to psychology than to anything else, especially as it is treated in Zen Buddhism.

When the masters declare: "Turn south and look at the polar star"; "The bridge flows but the water does not"; "The willow-leaves are not green, the flowers are not red"; etc., they are speaking in terms of their inner experience, and by this inner experience is meant the one which comes to us when mind and body dissolve, and by which all our ordinary ways of looking at the so-called world undergo some fundamental transformation. Naturally, statements issuing out of this sort of experience are full of contradictions and even appear altogether nonsensical. This is inevitable, but Zen finds its peculiar mission here.

What Indian Mahayana Sūtras state in abstract terms Zen does in concrete terms. Therefore, concrete individual images abound in Zen; in other words, Zen makes use, to a great extent, of poetical expressions; Zen is wedded to poetry.

In the beginning of Zen history, there was no specified method of studying Zen. Those who wished to understand it came to the master, but the latter had no stereotyped instruction to give, for this was impossible in the nature of things. He simply expressed in his own way either by gestures or in words his disapproval of whatever view his disciples might present to him, until he was fully satisfied with them. His dealing with his disciples was quite unique in the annals of spiritual exercises. He struck them with a stick, slapped them in the face, kicked them down to the ground; he gave an incoherent ejaculation, he laughed at them, made sometimes scornful, sometimes satirical, sometimes even abusive remarks, which will surely stagger those who are not used to the ways of a Zen master. This was not due to the irascible character of particular masters; it rather came out of the peculiar nature of the Zen experience, which, with all the means verbal and gesticulatory at his command, the master endeavours to communicate to his truth-seeking disciples. It was no easy task for them to understand this sort of communication. The point was, however, not to understand what came to them from the outside, but to awaken what lies within themselves. The master could not do anything further than indicate the way to it. In consequence of all this, there were not many who could readily grasp the teaching of Zen.

This difficulty, though inherent in the nature of Zen, was relieved a great deal by the development of the koan exercise in the eleventh century. This exercise has now become the special feature of Zen in Japan. Koan, literally meaning "official document," is a kind of problem given to Zen students for solution, which leads to the realisation of the truth of Zen. The koans are principally taken from the old masters' utterances. Now with a koan before the mind, the student knows where to fix his attention and to find the way to a realisation. Before this, he had to grope altogether in the dark, not knowing where to lay his hand in his search of a light.

The koan exercise is no doubt a great help to the understanding of Zen, but at the same time it is liable to lower the spiritual quality of the students who come to study Zen. Systematisation in one sense means popularisation, for things become easier to comprehend by being put in order. But this democratic diffusion tends to kill the chance for originality and creativeness, and these are the characteristics of the religious genius. System does not permit irregularities, they are generally excluded from it. But in Zen these irregular leapings are the thing most needed, although the koan exercise is a very flexible system and by the judicious use of it the master is able to educate his students in full accordance with the real spirit of Zen.

Zen came to Japan in the thirteenth century when the Kamakura government under the Hōjō family was having its heyday. It was at once embraced by the military class. Being direct and not requiring much learning, it was the very thing for the Hōjō warriors. Japanese culture under the Hōjō regime is noted for its austere simplicity, and for its vigorous creativeness, especially in religious thought: great Buddhist leaders were produced, who founded new schools of Buddhism; most Zen monasteries of the first importance were established; and the rise of Bushidō—the Warrior's Way—is coincident with the spread of Zen among the warrior class. The art of fencing too owes a great deal to the teaching of Zen, for it is deeply imbued with its mystic spirit. That the Japanese sword is to be used with both hands and that the Japanese warrior never carries a shield, always bending on attack, show how well the samurai appreciates the practice of Zen, in which the idea of "going-straight-ahead-ness"[6] is strongly emphasised.

Zen has had far more in Japan than in China to do with the moulding of the character of her people and the development of her culture. That is perhaps one of the reasons why Zen is still a living spiritual force in Japan, while in China it has almost ceased to be so. The Zendo (Meditation Hall) in Japan is visited by youths of character and intelligence, and that Zen tradition is very much a living fact is shown by the sale of books on Zen. Many devoted followers of Zen can be found among business men, statesmen, and other people of social importance. The Zendo is thus by no means an institution exclusively meant for the monks.

There are at present over twenty such institutions in Japan which belong to the Rinzai branch of Zen. In the Soto branch too there must be many, of which, however, I am not so well informed, and what is described in the following pages is principally applicable to the Rinzai. While both the Rinzai and the Soto belong to Zen, they have been differentiated from each other in the course of their history in China, but much more emphatically in Japan.

It is impossible, as I maintain, in the study of the Orient, especially in the study of Japanese character and culture, to neglect—much less to ignore—the influence of Zen. Zen ought to be studied not only in its theoretical aspect as a unique product of the Oriental mind, but in its practical aspect as is to be seen in the Zendo life. This is the chief motive for my writing this book, which is fully illustrated by Reverend Zenchū Sato, of Tōkeiji, Kamakura.

He is not a professional painter, but being one of those who have gone through all the disciplinary measures pertaining to the Zendo life, he is thoroughly imbued with its spirit, and what he has depicted here is the record of his own experience.

I have added many Zen "interviews" or "dialogues" or "stories" of the ancient masters culled somewhat at random from a work entitled Zen-rin Rui-shū in twenty fascicules. It is quite a handy book, giving Zen stories under classified headings; unfortunately, it is now a rare book.

DAISETZ TEITARO SUZUKI
Kamakura, January, 1934

Footnotes

1. Essays in Zen Buddhism, First Series, published 1927; Second Series, 1933; Third Series, 1934. Luzac and Company, London.
2. See my Zen Essays, Third Series, p. 207 ff.
3. Ibid., p. 1 ff. and p. 55 ff.
4. 639-713.
5. 686-760. One of Hui-nêng's principal disciples.
6. mo chili ch'u.

INITIATION

D.T. SUZUKI

MONK STARTING ON PILGRIMAGE PLATE 1

THE TRAINING OF the Zen monk takes place at the Semmon Dōjō which is the "seat of perfect wisdom" (bodhi-manda) specifically built for the purpose. While Dōjō has lost its original meaning and is nowadays used to designate any place of training, it still retains its primary connotation when it is applied to the Zen monastery.

Attached generally to all the principal Zen temples in Japan we find such a training station for the monks. A Zen monk is no Zen monk unless he goes through at least a few years of severe discipline at this institute. All the monks, therefore, who are ordained after the rite of the Zen school of Buddhism are supposed once in their life to enter here; with all their higher modern college education, no monks can have any ecclesiastical standing in their own circles if they were not once students of Zen here. They have thus every reason to come to the Semmon Dōjō and to submit themselves to its disciplinary curriculum.

As the writer at this moment of writing is living in the grounds of Engakuji, Kamakura, which is one of the main Zen monasteries in Japan, let him describe the Dōjō here. The monastery is surrounded by hills, and in one of the valleys along which one walks up to the higher and inner part of the grounds there is a temple called Shōzoku-in. The Semmon Dōjō is inside the gate of this temple, which comprises, as we have it at present, the tomb of the founder of Engakuji, the hall dedicated to him, the hall enshrining the Buddha's Sarīra (in the classical style of Sung architecture), the Zendo (i.e., meditation hall), the Shōzoku-in itself (constituting the Joju part of the monastery), the belfry, and the residential quarters of the Master known as Zempanryō or Inryō. Most buildings here are reconstructions since the earthquake of 1923. Let us imagine that all the scenes to be depicted in the following pages are with more or less exactitude referred to a Semmon Dōjō somewhat resembling the one in the Engakuji monastery, while the pictures themselves may often remind the reader of one of the Kyoto Semmon Dōjō if he has ever been resident there.

The life at the Semmon Dōjō, which, by way of abbreviation, will be later spoken of as the Zendo life, is something altogether out of keeping with modern life. We can almost say that anything modern and many things ordinarily regarded as symbolic of a pious life are absent here. Instead of labour-saving machinery, what may appear as labour-wasting is encouraged. Commercialism and self advertisement are banned. Scientific, intellectual education is interdicted. Comfort, luxury, and womanly kindness are conspicuous for their absence. There is, however, a spirit of grim earnestness, with which higher truths are sought; there is determined devotion to the attainment of superior wisdom, which will help to put an end to all the woes and ailments of human life, and also to the acquirement of the fundamental social virtues, which quietly pave the way to world-peace and the promotion of the general welfare of all humankind. The Zen life thus aims, besides maturing the monk's spiritual development, at turning out good citizens as social members as well as individuals.

The Zendo life may be roughly analysed into (1) life of humility, (2) life of labour, (3) life of service, (4) life of prayer and gratitude, and (5) life of meditation. After his initiation to the Brotherhood, the monk is to be trained along these lines.

By "initiation" is meant a monk's being taken into the

communal body of a Zen Brotherhood connected with a given monastery. This presenting himself as a noviciate requires some preliminary steps. He must first be provided with a certificate as a regularly ordained disciple of a Zen priest, and then he is to be equipped with all the articles which belong to the make-up of a monk travelling for the study of Zen. The articles a monk needs are very few in number, and easily carried by him over the shoulders. With a bamboo hat, deep and large, over his head and a pair of straw-sandals and cotton leggings securely protecting his legs and feet, the monk appears before the porch of the Dōjō.

This travelling or pilgriming[1] which is technically known as angya (hsing-chiao, "going on foot") has a special significance for the monk, and even when every form of modern transportation is available, he has to dress himself in the complete travelling attire as in ancient days and thus to present himself before the Dōjō authorities (Plate 1). Here is the "Song of Angya" composed by Shan-chao of Fên-yang, (Funnyo Zensho), one of the noted Chinese Zen masters of the early Sung:

"Determined to leave his parents, what does he want to accomplish?
He is a Buddhist, a homeless monk now, and no more a man of the world;
His mind is ever intent on the mastery of the Dharma.
"His conduct is to be as transparent as ice or a crystal,
His is not to seek fame and wealth,
He is to rid himself of defilements of all sorts.
"He has no other way open to him but to go about and inquire;
Let him be trained in mind and body by walking over the mountains and fording the rivers;
Let him befriend wise men in the Dharma and pay them

respect wherever he may accost them;
Let him brave the snow, tread on the frosty roads, not minding the severity of the weather;
Let him cross the waves and penetrate the clouds, chasing away dragons and evil spirits.
"His iron staff accompanies him wherever he travels and his copper pitcher is well filled,
Let him not then be annoyed with the longs and shorts of worldly affairs,
His friends are those in the monastery with whom he may weigh the Dharma,
Trimming off once for all the four propositions and one hundred negations.
"Beware of being led astray by others to no purpose whatever;
Now that you are in the monastery your business is to walk the great path,
And not to get attached to the world, but to be empty of all trivialities;
Holding fast on to the ultimate truth do not refuse hard working in any form;
Cutting yourself away from noise and crowds, stop all your toiling and craving.
"Thinking of the one who threw himself down the precpice, and the one who stood all night in the snow, gather up all your fortitude,
So that you may keep the glory of your Dharma-king manifested all the time;
Be ever studious in the pursuit of the Truth, be ever reverential towards the Elders;
You are asked to stand the cold and the heat and privations,
Because you have not yet come to the abode of peace;

Cherish no envious thoughts for worldly prosperity, be not depressed just because you are slighted;
But endeavour to see directly into your own nature, not depending on others.
"Over the five lakes and the four seas you pilgrim from monastery to monastery;
To walk thousands of miles over hundreds of mountains is indeed no easy task;
May you finally intimately interview the master in the Dharma and be led to see into your own nature,
When you will no more take weeds for the medicinal plants."

Travelling nowadays is done by railways or air-line, and all the charm, all the experience, and all the education one gets from travelling on foot as in ancient days are entirely lost—which is one of the great moral losses we moderns sustain in this mechanical age. When mountain-climbing is made too easy, the spiritual effect the mountain exercises vanishes into the air. The moral benefit the modern monk thus forgoes together with the picturesqueness of his life is to be greatly regretted. We must somehow find ways—the sooner the better—to compensate all such losses inevitably arising from science, machine, and capitalism.

In whichever way we may travel, on foot or by train, life itself is a form of angya: "Whence?" is the name of our starting station and "Whither?" is that of the arrival. Hence this admonition by Ta-hui[2] given to one of his lay-disciples:
"Whence is birth? Whither is death? He who knows this

'Whence and Whither' is said to be the true Buddhist. But who is the one that knows birth and death? Who is the one that suffers birth and death? Who is the one that does not know whence birth is and whither death is? Who is the one that suddenly comes to the realisation of this 'Whence and Whither'? When this is not thoroughly understood, the eyes rove, the heart palpitates, the viscera writhe, as if a fire-ball were rolling up and down inside the body. And who is the one, again, that undergoes this torture? If you want to know who this one is, dive down into the depths of your being, where no intellection is possible to reach; and when you know it, you know that there is a place where neither birth nor death can touch."

The object of the Zen monk's pilgrimage as well as that of our life-*angya*, is to come to the understanding of all these questions set up by Ta-hui; for this is "seeing into one's own nature". Mere visiting one holy sight after another is not in the programme of the Zen travelling, angya.

As Life carries its own bundle in the form of the body, so does the monk carry a travelling bundle over his shoulders. How happy we might be—so we imagine quite frequently indeed—if we were freed from this inevitable "bundle" known as the body or the flesh! As this is impossible, all we could do is perhaps to reduce the amount and weight of the bundle to a minimum. The less the bundle the freer will be our movement. For this reason, the monk limits his luggage to the contents of a papier-mache box about 13 x 10 x 3½ inches called kesa-bunko. In it we find a priestly robe (kesa = kaṣāya), a razor, the home address, some money (which is to be used for burial in case of his unexpected death), a book or two, a set of bowls (which are tied outside to the box), and other little miscellaneous things.

The worst passion we mortals cherish is the desire to

possess. Even when we know that our final destination is a hole not more than three feet square, we have the strongest craving for accumulation, which we cannot ourselves make any use of after death. The monk mutely protests against this human passion by limiting his possessions to the last degree.

In ancient days when there was yet no railway travelling, the monk had to pass many nights on his way to the monastery where he decided to study Zen. Since he had no money, those nights were to be spent under any shelter he would come across, generally in a Buddhist temple where hospitality was most generously extended, but, if such was not available, in the open field or in a lonely roadside shrine. This was indeed a good practical education for the young monk who has now decided to give final solution to the questions, as were formulated by Ta-hui, but which, really, have been stirred deep in his own heart. For the questions are to be solved, if they are at all solved, by keeping a close contact with life. When this contact is lost, the questions become subjects of intellection. The young monk must, therefore, experience life in its hardest and toughest aspects; unless he suffers he cannot probe into the depths of his own being. Travelling teaches this, and it was well for him to be prepared for all that might be coming to him in his monkish pilgrimage.

He has now arrived at his destination. The picture (Plate 2) shows the entrance to the temple which is attached to the Zendo. One of the monk-officials has come out to see the new applicant. The latter respectfully presents his letter of introduction and a certificate from his master by whom he was

ASKING FOR ADMITTANCE PLATE 2

ordained. But he is politely but firmly refused acceptance to the Brotherhood. The plea is conventional these days: the Zendo is too full, or the temple is too poor, and no more admittance is possible. If the monk-novice accepts this quietly and tries another monastery, there will be no Zendo where he can find entrance; for he will everywhere meet this form of refusal.

The refusal is given once and the official withdraws. Being left alone, the monk has now nothing else to do but to continue his supplication in the same attitude as was assumed in the beginning: he leans over his baggage with his head down. He is fortunate if he is left to himself thus undisturbed. For he is sometimes forcibly ejected as an obstinate monk who refuses to accept the decision given out to him by the Brotherhood.

When the Zen monks want to be rude, they can be so. The new persistent applicant is now rejected by force from the entrance and pushed outside the gate which is closed behind him. He will not, however, be dismayed; he spreads his seat, lets down his bundle, and begins to sit cross-legged; before long he may be found apparently deeply absorbed in meditation. The night advances, and the moon is seen going down between the branches of a tree (Plate 3).

It seems as if no soft spots were left in the heart of the Zen master. What he generally doles out to his monks is "hot invective and angry fist-shaking". For the Zen truth is something which must be snatched away from the hands of the master; he will never be too ready to bestow it mildly on those who beg. He is to be made willy nilly to hand it to them. This is where the Zen discipline differs from other religious trainings. We will have further occasions to see how this is.

D.T. SUZUKI

ADMITTANCE REFUSED PLATE 3

As is mostly the case, the "new arrival" (shin-tō) will be invited in when the evening comes. He is then at least for one night assured of being sheltered from exposure; but if he expects to sleep under a warm bedding, he will be terribly disappointed. No such accommodations are waiting him, and he is ready to stand all trials. He has been informed of all these inconveniences before he started on this pilgrimage. Zen monks are not supposed to pass their nights lying comfortably in bed; when the questions baffling all intellectual attempts at solution are still harassing them, how can they hope to have any kind of rest? There were many examples in the annals of Zen, which they may follow if they really want to be enlightened. Tzu-ming (Jimyo) of the Sung pierced his thigh with a drill when he felt sleepy while meditating. The new arrival passes his nights facing the wall in the posture of meditation (Plate 4). When the morning comes, he puts on his straw-sandals, goes out, and nods his head over his own baggage as he did on the previous day.

This period of probation, otherwise called niwa-dzume, "occupying the entrance court," may last at least two or three days—which formerly extended even to a week. This spending all day with the head down on the bundle is, to say the least, a most tiresome and trying procedure. How high his ideal and how exalted his aspirations, the Zen monk without the sense of humility and self-abnegation is not expected to attain the highest degree of purification. This niwa-dzume is the first practical lesson given to him as soon as he arrives at the Zendo.

After the niwa-dzume comes what is known as tangwa-

NIGHT IN THE LODGING ROOM PLATE 4

dzume. Tangwa literally means "to leave in the morning" and is the name given to the room where travelling monks are given a night's lodging; they are not allowed to stay for a second night, hence the name. The monk-novice is now allowed to come inside and pass another three days' probation period in this room. Thus left in solitary confinement, as it were, he passes all day in meditation.

When about five days are passed since the arrival at the monastery, the novice monk gets a notice from the office known as Shika-ryō, which is the directing centre of the whole Brotherhood.

According to the notice, he is to be at last permitted into the Zendo. He is told about the regulations, and good sound advice is given to him by the head-monk. In the following morning after breakfast he is transferred from the lodging room' to the Zendo. He puts on his kesa, which is the formal ceremonial robe for all the Buddhist priesthood. He is ushered by one of the monks in charge of the Zendo, first to pay respect to Mañjuśrī the Bodhisattva, who is enshrined near the front entrance. Spreading his zagu which is a square piece of silk with a design, he prostrates himself three times before him (Plate 5). When this is done, he is led to his own seat where he finds his humble baggage leaning against the window. As he takes it, the usher-monk in a loud voice announces the admission of a new member into the Brotherhood. A tea-ceremony follows, and the novice monk begins his Zendo life.

The novice has not yet been presented to the master himself—this takes place a few days later. One morning he

INITIATED TO THE ZENDO PLATE 5

THE SECRET WORLD OF THE ZEN BUDDHIST MONK

is told to have his "interview incense" in readiness, which is to be offered to the Rōshi, that is, the master. Incense is used for various purposes in the monastery. In this case, incense-offering is a kind of pledge that this newly-admitted one takes in good faith the present master for his instructor in Zen. At the threshold of the master's room, the monk spreads his "seat-cloth" (zagu) and on it bows three times. In the meantime the master folds his hands before him (Plate 6). "Tea ceremony" is partaken by both, which consists in just drinking tea each out of his cup. The Rōshi is likely to ask the monk concerning his name, native place, education, etc.

The first interview may end with this kind of conversation, since the monk is a perfect novice in Zen. Anciently, however, even the initial interview between a new arrival and the master went directly into the heart of the matter, and something like the following took place:

Hsüeh-fêng (Seppo) asked a monk, "What is your name?"
Monk: "My name is Hsüan-chi" (literally "Mysterious Loom").
Seppo: "How much cloth do you weave everyday?"
Monk: "Not a piece of cloth I have on me."
Seppo: "Go back to your Zendo."
Before the monk took a few steps to leave the master's presence, the latter called out: "Your kesa (priestly robe) is dropping on the ground!"
The monk turned his head, whereupon Seppo said: "Fine that you have not a piece of cloth over you!"
Han-chu (Ganshu) asked a monk: "Wang and Huang, Li and Chao—these are not your original family names; what is your original one?"
Monk: "Same as yours."
Ganshu: "Let alone being of the same family; I want to know your original family name."

D.T. SUZUKI

INTRODUCED TO ROSHI PLATE 6

Monk: "When the River Han reverses its downward course, I will tell you."
Ganshu: "Why not now?"
Monk: "Has the River reversed its course, or not?" Ganshu was satisfied with the monk.

Wên of Chên-ching (Shinjō Bun) asked a monk: "Where do you come from?"
Monk: "From Ta-yang (Daigyo)."
Bun: "Where did you pass your last summer sojourn?"
Monk: "Ta-kuei (Dai-yi)."
Bun: "Where is your native place?"
Monk: "Hsing-yüan Fu (Kōgenfu)."
Extending his hand now, Bun said: "How is it that my hand is so much like the Buddha's hand?"
The monk did not know how to take it. Said the master: "So far your answers have been splendidly natural and easy; and what obstructions do you feel now that I ask about my hand resembling the Buddha's?"
Monk: "I fail to perceive the point."
Master: "All is perfectly open to you, and there is nothing specially for you to perceive."
Thus commented on, the monk at once had his obstructions removed.

Our novice-monk has not yet had his koan, and we must wait until he has solved his first one when he will be able to understand these "dialogues." At the time of the evening sanzen, he is told to come to the Rōshi with the rest, and then he will have his koan, which means the real beginning of his Zendo life.

Footnotes

1 It is possible that the usage originally started from Sudhana's visit, as related in the gandhanavyuha, to more than fifty masters in various walks of life.
2. Ta-hui was one of the greatest characters in the Sung history of Zen.

LIFE OF HUMILITY

WHILE THERE IS no doubt that the chief means of supporting the Zendo life is begging, as was in the ancient days of the Buddha, begging has, besides its economic value, a twofold moral signification: the one is to teach the beggar humility and the other is to make the donor accumulate the merit of self-denial. Both have a great social value when they are understood in their proper bearings, and what is most strongly emphasised in the monk's life is this social meaning, and not necessarily its economic importance. For if it were necessary to support themselves by some other means, the monastery authorities would soon have found the way for it. But on account of its educative value begging has been selected for the monks to be the chief method of maintaining themselves physically. On certain days the monks all go out forming a long line and walk slowly in the streets, crying "Hō." (Plate 7). Each of them carries a bowl, in which he receives money or rice. The offering is thanked for with a short recitation. Generally, however, the monks go out in a small company of four or five. They all wear deep broad hats which permit the wearer to see only three or four feet ahead. They cannot even notice the face of the donor who may drop a cent in their bowl. This is purposely done. The donor is not to know who the beggar is, nor does the beggar observe who the donor is. The deed of charity is to be practised altogether free from personal relationships. When the latter are present, the deed is apt to lose its spiritual sense. It is just an act of favouritism, that is, it harbours in it on the one side the feeling of personal superiority and on the other the degrading consciousness of subserviency.

The bowl the monks carry has figured very much in the

D.T. SUZUKI

TAKUHATSU-ING IN THE STREETS PLATE 7

history of Zen. Together with the "robe" it symbolises priestly authority. When Hui-nêng (Yenō) had an insight into the truth of Zen, his master, Hung-jên (Gunin) is said to have handed his own robe and bowl[1] over to Hui-nêng in order to testify that his disciple had the correct understanding of Zen. Later, one of Hung-jên's disciples wanted to carry the bowl away from Hui-nêng. Hui-nêng made no special efforts to resist the intruder, but for some mysterious reason the latter could not lift the bowl. Later the Emperor Tai-tsung of Sung held up a monk's bowl in his hands, and asked Wang Sui, his minister: "Once at Tai-yu Ling the bowl was not to be lifted up, and how is it that it is now securely in my hands?" The minister failed to answer the Imperial question.

When Nan-ch'üan (Nansen) saw one of his monks washing a bowl, he took it away from him. The monk stood empty-handed. Thereupon Ch'üan remarked: "The bowl is in my hands, and what is the use of making so much talk about it?"

While Hsüeh-fêng (Seppa) was staying at the Kuo-ch'ing monastery, he held up his bowl and said to a Buddhist scholar: "When you understand the Truth, this will be given to you."
Scholar: "Such transaction is the business of a
Transformation Buddha."
Fêng: "You are not worthy even of being a servant to a Buddhist scholar."
Scholar: "I fail to understand."
Fêng: "You ask me then, and I will give you the answer."
When the scholar was about to make a bow, Feng kicked him down to the ground.
Later, the Buddhist scholar came to Yün-mên (Ummon) and said: "It took me seven years to see into the meaning."
Mên: "Did it really?"
Scholar: "Yes, indeed."
Mên: "Another seven years may have to elapse before it

fully becomes yours."

To see into the meaning of Zen is not enough; it must be thoroughly assimilated into every fibre of one's existence; and to do this fourteen years' constant application cannot be said to be too arduous a task. In fact, the Zen monk has to pass about that length of time in the Zendo before he is fully qualified as a Zen master.

Attached to a Zendo there are generally many householders who regularly contribute so much rice towards the maintenance of the institution. To collect such offerings, the monks are detailed to go out once a month. Each carries a bag over his shoulders, and visits the donors' houses one after another; when the bag is filled with rice, it proves to be quite a heavy load, especially when he has to walk along the muddy or pebbly country road in a storm back to his monastery.

Anciently, there was a monk, who, thus equipped, visited a householder. The monk was bitten by a dog. The householder said, "When a dragon puts on even a piece of cloth over him, it is said that no Garuda will ever dare attack him. You are wrapped up in the monk's robe, and yet you have been hurt by a dog: why is this so ?"

It is not mentioned what reply was given by the monk mendicant.

Wang the court-official once asked a monk: "All beings are endowed with the Buddha-nature; is it really so?"

Monk: "Yes, it is."

Wang pointed at the picture of a dog on the wall and said: "Is this, too, supplied with the Buddha-nature?"

The monk did not know what to say. Whereupon the official gave the answer for him:

"Look out, the dog bites!"

The monk and the dog have been associated in a strange way from the early days of Zen history in China. The koan

"Mu!" or "Wu!" which is the "iron bull" given to all the Zen monks to chew thoroughly, is no other than Chao-chou's (Jōshū) answer to the question: "Is the dog endowed with the Buddha-nature ?" Even when out in the collecting tour, the monk is accosted by the dog (Plate 8).

In the autumn the monks go out in the country when the farmers are ready to gather up pumpkins, daikons, potatoes, turnips, and other vegetables. They ask for such as are rejected by the farmers as unfit for the market. When they have enough collected they pile them on a hand-cart which is pulled by them as far as the foot of the hill where the monastery is situated. After that, the load will be carried on their backs up to the kitchen, and then some will be made ready for immediate consumption while others will be used for pickles or preserved for winter supply (Plate 9).

Footnote

1. What was really handed to Hui-nêng was the robe only, but later somehow the bowl came to be mentioned along with the robe.

D.T. SUZUKI

MONTHLY COLLECTION OF RICE PLATE 8

TAKUHATSU-ING FOR DAIKON PLATE 9

LIFE OF LABOR

"*A* DAY OF NO work is a day of no eating" is the literal rendering of the first rule of the monastery life. Pai-chang (720-814), who was the founder of the Zendo institution, was always found together with his monks engaged in some manual work. The monks wanted to keep him away because they did not wish to see their old master working as hard as themselves. But he insisted, "I have accumulated no merit to deserve service by others; if I do not work, I have no right to take my meal." His motive of work evidently came from his feeling of humility, but in fact manual labour forms one of the most essential features of the Zen life. In India, the monks simply begged for their food and were not inclined to work hard. But things were different in China. Life meant to the Chinese monks to be engaged in physical labour, to move their hands and feet, to handle tools, in order to accomplish some visible and tangible ends. This practicalness of the Chinese mind saved Buddhism from sinking into a state of lethargy and a life of mere contemplation, as we see this fact emphatically verified in the life of the Zen monastery.

However high and soaring to the sky our ideas may be, we are firmly fixed to the earth; there is no way of escaping this physical existence. Whatever thoughts we may have, they must definitely be related to our body, if they are to have the power to influence life in any way. The Zen monk is asked to solve highly abstract metaphysical problems; and to do this he devotes himself to meditation. But as long as this meditation remains identified with abstractions, there will be no practical solution of the problems. The Yogin may think he has clearly seen into this meaning . But when this does not go beyond his hours of meditation, that is, when it is not actually put to experiment in his daily life, the solution is merely ideational, it bears no fruits, and therefore it dies out before long. Zen masters have, therefore, always been anxious to see their monks work hard on the farm, in the woods, or in the mountains (Plates 10,11,12). In fact, they themselves would lead the labouring party, taking up the spade, the scissors, or the axe, or carrying water, or pulling the cart.

There was also a democratic spirit here in action. The term puch'ing, "all-invited", means to have every member of the Brotherhood on the field. No distinctions are made, no exemptions are allowed; for the high as well as the low in the hierarchy are engaged in the same kind of work. There is a division of labour, naturally, but no social class-idea inimical to the general welfare of the community.

The history of Zen abounds with allusions to the master actually in the midst of some physical labour when a monk comes and asks him a question.

A monk caught Chao-chou in the act of sweeping when he proposed this question: "You are a great Zen master free from the dust of evil thoughts, and why this busy sweeping?" "The dust comes from outside"—came quickly from the master.

Chao-chou was once keeper of fire (huo t'ou) at a certain monastery. One day closing up the gate, he made a fire and filled the house with smoke. He went on loudly crying, "Fire! Fire!" The entire Brotherhood was astir and rushed up to the gate which they found closed, and there was no way of getting inside. Chao-chou said, "If you can say a word, the gate will be opened." The monks were taken aback and no words were forthcoming. Nanch'üan who was among the crowd, however, took out the key and passed it over to Chao-chou through the window. With it Chao-chou opened the gate.

THE SECRET WORLD OF THE ZEN BUDDHIST MONK

WOOD-GATHERING PLATE 10

SWEEPING PLATE 11

GARDENING PLATE 12

Chih-chang, of Kuei-tsung, (Kisu Chijō), one day went out to the monastery farm to pick some vegetables. He drew a circle around some herbs, and said to the monks not to disturb them. The monks were careful not to touch them. After a while the master came out again in the yard, and seeing the herbs untouched he chased all the monks with a stick and said, "O this company of fools! Not one of them has enough intelligence!"

Hsüeh-Feng once asked Chang-ch'ing (Chōkei) who came up to see the master in his room, "What is that?" said Chang, "Fine weather, just the day for general outdoor work (pu-ch'ing)

Another time seeing a monk pass by, Hsüeh-feng beckoned him to approach and asked, "Where are you going?" The monk answered, "I am going to join the 'general work' (pu-ch'ing)." Said the master, "Then, go!"

Yüeh-an (Gettan) once asked Lien, of Yü-ch'üan, about Yün-mên's excusing Tung-shan (Dōzan) for thirty blows which Shan deserved.[1] But Lien failed to give An a satisfactory answer. One day he joined a general work party (pu-ch'ing). When he came up to the Mi-t'o Ling with a load of rice on his back, he was thoroughly exhausted. He set the load down on the ground, drawing a long breath. This unexpectedly opened his mind to the meaning of the koan previously challenged. He exclaimed, "How happy I am!" Later when he saw Yüeh-an, An said, "You now believe that I never deceived you."

Yüeh-shan (Yakusan) one day seeing the monk-gardener planting vegetables said to him:

"Very well with your planting, but don't let the roots grow."

The monk protested, "If the roots fail to grow, what has our Brotherhood to eat?"

"Have you a mouth to eat?" queried the master.

No answer came from the gardener.

When Yün, of Shih-mên, was working as head-gardener

at Ch'ing-lin, Lin the master asked:
"What are you going to do today?"
Yün: "I am going to plant vegetables."
Lin: "The Buddha-body fills the entire universe and where do you find a patch of ground to plant your seeds?"
Yün: "No sooner the golden spade moves than the holy plants begin to grow everywhere."
The following day Lin came out on the farm and called to Yün the gardener. The latter replied, "Yes, master." Lin suggested: "Let us plant a shadowless tree for the sake of posterity."
Yün: "If it is a shadowless one, it will never suffer our plantation."
Lin: "We won't talk about whether it suffers our plantation, or not; have you ever seen its branches, its leaves?"
Yün: "No, never yet!"
Lin: "If you have never seen them, how can you know that it will not suffer our plantation?"
Yün: "Just because I have never seen them, I say that it will not suffer our plantation."
Lin: "Yes, so it is, so it is."
While Hsüeh-feng was at Tung-shan he was carrying a bundle of kindlings which he set down before Shan. Shan asked: "How heavy is it?"
Fêng: "Even when all the people of the world try to lift it, they cannot."
Shan: "How then has it come up so far?"
Hsüan-sha Pei (Gensha Shibi) said to his monks, who were all employed with him in carrying fuel: "You are all sharing my power." One of the monks said, "If we are all sharing your power, what need is there for us to be engaged thus in this general work?" The master gave him a scolding, saying, "If not for this general work, how can we come home all loaded with fuel?"

Chang, of Hsi-slian used to be the head wood-chopper at T'ou-tzü-shan, and later came to Hsüeh-fêng. Fêng said, "Are you not Chang the wood-chopper?" Chang at once raised his arms and swung them as if chopping wood with an axe. Fêng nodded his head.

Ch'êng, of Ti-t'sang, was found one day working on the paddy-field. Seeing a novice-monk corning his way, he asked, "Where do you come from?"

Monk: "From the south."

Ch'ên: "How is Buddhism faring in the south?"

Monk: "Discussions on the spiritual subjects are going on fine."

Ch'ên: "With all their discussions on Zen, there is nothing there comparable to our cultivating the field, gathering crops, and eating boiled rice."

Monk: "What about the triple world?"

Ch'ên: "What do you mean by the triple world?"

The monk had no words to say.

When Mi, of Shen-shan was working with Tung-shan on the tea-garden, Tung let down his hoe, saying, "I am all tired out, no energy whatever is left in me."

Mi: "If there were no energy left, how could you even say that?"

Tung: "You thought there was one with enough energy, did you not?"

Mi did not pursue him any further.

Shêng, of Yŭn-yên was hoeing on the ginger farm, when Tao-wu came up to him and asked: "You are just hoeing this one, but can you hoe the other one?" Shêng retorted, "Bring me the other one."

As we may see from these Zen dialogues, the masters as well as the monks were equally employed in all kinds of manual labour, which were needed in their monastery life. Nothing was regarded as mean and below their dignity, for they were perfectly aware of the deep meaning in everything they did, whether with their hands or with their minds. There was no dualistic discrimination in their way of thinking and feeling. Otherwise, all these dialogues could not have taken place while they were thus working in the field or inside the monastery buildings. The dialogues or discussions were most intimately connected with life itself. Each pulsation of the heart, the lifting of the hands and feet-all evoked considerations of a most serious character. For this is the only way to study Zen and to live it. Nothing can ever really be learned until it works through the nerves and muscles. Pai-chang was a great Zen master who had a wonderful insight into the working of human psychology. If not for him, Zen as we have it might never have come into existence. In this respect we owe a great deal to the Chinese genius.

The monks are not always hard-working farmers and labourers; they often have free energy left for physical sports. When they are exempt from the daily routine work, they entertain themselves by planning wrestling matches, which is one of the great national sports of Japan (Plate 13). It goes without saying that in this the principle of fair play is most scrupulously observed.

Footnote

1. Zen Essays, III. Pp. 135-6.

WRESTLING PLATE 13

LIFE OF SERVICE

*T*HE GOVERNMENT OF the Zendo life is entrusted to the hands of the senior members of the Brotherhood. Their offices are generally: Tenzo-ryo which looks after food supplies and prepares them for the monks: Densu-ryo which attends to all the affairs connected with the Buddha shrine; Shika-ryō which is a kind of general directing office; Fusu-ryo which keeps accounts; Yinji-ryō which attends on the master known as Rōshi; Jisha-ryō which looks after the Holy Monk as well as the Zendo; etc. Generally the offices change twice a year.

To serve as a cook in the Zendo life means that the monk has attained some understanding about Zen, for it is one of the positions highly honoured in the monastery, and may be filled only by one of those who have passed a number of years here. The work is quite an irksome one, and, besides, a kind of underground service which is not very much noticed by superficial observers (Plate 14). Just because of this, to be the cook in the monastery affords the monks a good opportunity "to accumulate merit" which is turned over to their own attainment of Sarvajñatā as well as its universal realisation. The meaning of service is to do the work assigned ungrudgingly and without thought of personal reward material or moral. The only desire the worker cherishes in the execution of his service is to turn its merit to the general treasure-house of All knowledge (Sarvajñatā).

The main problem with the cook will then be to make

COOKING PLATE 14

the best possible use of the food material given to him for the maintenance of health among the members of the Brotherhood. There is naturally nothing very appealing to the sense of a gourmand in the Zendo pantry, but cooking may to a great extent be improved by a judicious use of shōyu or miso. The high-browed ones are generally apt to despise this kind of work as below their dignity whatever the term may mean. But with the monks there is nothing low or high in their work. If they could have chances to do good to others in any way they might come across, they should be willing to avail themselves of them and do the work assigned to them to the best of their abilities. The training at the Zendo is not only for the development of a man's inner psychic powers but for that of his moral character as a social being.

> K'ai, of Ch'ing-yin, was a cook at T'ou-tzu. The master of T'ou-tzŭ said, "It is no easy task to work as a cook like this."
> K'ai: "It is very kind of you."
> Master: "Is your office to boil gruel, or to steam rice?"
> K'ai: "The one helper rinses rice and starts the fire, while the other boils gruel and steams rice."
> Master: "What is your work then?"
> K'ai: "Through your kindness I have nothing to do but idle away my time."

Had K'ai really no work to do as a cook? Was he just passing his time idly? How then could he be detailed as cook? In the Zendo life deep problems for solution are lying everywhere, and the master is ever ready to pick them up and make the monks face them.

One of the principles governing the life at Zendo, as was elsewhere alluded to, is not to waste. This applies with special emphasis to cookery where the vegetables or grains of rice and barley are always liable to be thoughtlessly thrown away. Chu, of Shih Shuang who acted as keeper of the granary at Kuei-shan, was one day found putting rice through a sieve, when the master of the Kuei-shan monastery appeared and said: "Don't scatter the grains for they come from our kind-hearted donors."

Chu: "No, master, I won't scatter them about."

The master looked around and picked up a grain of rice from the ground and said: "You say you don't scatter them about; if so, where does this grain come from?"

Chu remained silent; the master continued: "Be careful not to think slightingly of this one grain of rice, for hundreds of thousands of grains all come out of it."

Chu: "May I ask where this one grain comes from?"

The master made no special answer to this, but laughing heartily went back to his own quarters. In the evening he came out into the Hall and said: "O monks, there is a worm in our rice."

Eating is a solemn affair in the Zendo life, though there is not much to eat. The best meal called saiza or otoki which takes place about ten o'clock in the morning consists of rice mixed with barley, miso soup, and pickles. The breakfast is gruel and pickles, while the supper is what is left of the saiza. Properly speaking, the Zen monks are supposed to eat only twice a day after the fashion set up by the Buddha in India. The evening meal is, therefore, called yaku-seki, "medicinal food." The modes of living are to be adjusted to climatic conditions.

When they are all seated, the Prajñāpāramitā-hṛdaya-sūtra (Shingyo) is recited, the ten Buddha-names are invoked:

Vairocana Buddha as the Dharmakāya pure and undefiled; Locana Buddha as the perfected Sambhogakāya; Śākyamuni Buddha as one of the innumerable Nirmāṇakāyas; Maitreya Buddha who will descend among us in the time to come; all the Buddhas of the past, present, and future, in all the ten quarters; Mañjuśrī the Bodhisattva of Great Wisdom; Samantabhadra the Bodhisattva of Great Deed; Avalokiteśvara the Bodhisattva of Great Love; all the venerable Bodhisattva-Mahāsattvas; and Mahāprajñā-pāramitā. After this, if it is breakfast, the virtues of rice gruel are recounted; if it is dinner, the prayer is offered that the meal be equally shared by all sentient beings including the denizens of the spiritual worlds. The five subjects of meditation are then repeated: (1) Do we really merit this offering? (2) We are seriously made to think about our own virtues; (3) The object is to detach ourselves from the fault of greed and other defects; (4) Meal is to be taken as medicine in order to keep the body healthy and strong; (5) We accept this meal so as to make ourselves fit receptacles for the truth. The Five Meditations are followed by these vows: The first morsel is for destroying all evils; the second morsel is for practising all deeds of goodness; the third morsel is for delivering all beings so that we all finally attain Buddhahood[1] (Plate 15).

No words are uttered during the course of eating, everything goes on silently and in the most orderly sequence. The waiters are monks themselves taking their turn. When finished, the head-monk claps the wooden blocks. The bowls are quietly washed at the table and wiped and put up in a piece of cloth which is carried by each monk. While this is going on, some verses are recited. When the hand-bell is struck, the diners all stand and walk back to their hall in perfect order.

D.T. SUZUKI

DINING ROOM PLATE 15

When a monk is sick and cannot stand the Zendo life, he is taken into a separate room called Enjudo ("life-prolonging room") where he is nursed by a fellow-monk. It is thus that the young novice begins to learn how to serve his fellow-monks. (Plate 16). In graver cases the patient will of course be sent to a hospital where he is with due care looked after.

Even while sick, the monk is not to release himself from spiritual exertion; he is always made to think of the masters and their ways of dealing with the problem—the problem of human ills which befall us most annoyingly in multitude of forms.

Why was Vimalakīrti (Yuima) sick? To the inquiry made by Mañjuśrī he said, "He was sick because of all beings, who were constantly suffering from ignorance and anger and passion." But, according to the Prajñāpāramita, the Bodhisattva is not to become frightened about sickness because there is no such thing as sickness in the realm of Sarvajñatā. Why is this? Let us see how the ancient Zen masters handled the problem.

The most noted case recorded in the history of Zen is that of Ma-tsu (Baso) the great teacher of Zen. When he was ill, the keeper of the temple asked: "How do you feel these days?" He answered: "Oh, the Sun-faced Buddha! The Moon-faced Buddha!"

Yün-mên (Ummon) asked a monk: "What is your business now?"
Monk: "Nursing the sick."
Master: "Do you know that there is one who never gets sick?"

NURSING THE SICK PLATE 16

Monk: "I do not understand."
Master: "Whether you say 'yes,' or whether you say 'no,' it is all the same—'I do not understand.'"
The monk was silent.
Master: "You ask me."
Monk: "Who is it that never becomes sick?"
The master pointed at a monk who happened to be near him.

Shun, of Pai-yang, was out of sorts for some time and gave out the following to his monks:

"Afflicted with illness I have not been able to lift my head from the wooden pillow.
Visitors are many and varied, asking me how I am;
In response to inquiries, various in nature and form, I have given my answers,
While the nightingale before my window more busily chatters away its praise of the spring.

"Let those of you who are able to answer as regards the source of my illness come forward and point out for me where in this body seven ch'ih long lies this trouble of mine."

The monks tried to answer the question, but none were found satisfactory. Thereupon, the master himself gave this for answer: He stroked the palm of his hand and opening his mouth made the movement as if to vomit. An other answer of his was: "What a fine pillow this!"

Hsin, of Huang-lung, one day noticed his head-monk laid up with a cold. He sent his attendant to his sick-chamber with this question: "Has your cold come from within, or from without? If it has entered from without, you have no pain inside; if it has come out of yourself, you are not hurt anywhere outwardly. Where does it come from, anyway?" The sick monk's reply was: "The monk finds his night-lodging at the monastery; the robber does not break into the poor man's house." Hsin, however, refused to approve of it, and gave his own answer: "See how the nose flows!" Or, "The head aches and the eyes are watery."

Certain dates are set apart for the purpose of washing soiled clothes, patching underwears, and curing the aching body by moxa burning. The latter is one of the ancient Oriental methods of healing the tired body. After working hard on the farm, or walking to the distant villages to beg for rice, or sitting for a long time cross legged on the cushion, intently meditating on a koan, the monk is sure to ache all over the body, perhaps particularly in the legs. In such cases the burning of the moxa herb on some definitely specified spots of the body is considered quite effective to cure the pain or strain. The cauterisation of the skin seems in some unknown way to help the even circulation of the blood. The choosing of the spots where the treatment is most beneficial is left to the experts. But some of the spots are known generally to us, and the monk is quite an adept in this (Plate 17).

As the monk washes and mends his own clothes, he becomes a great expert in this after one or two years' stay at the Zendo. He also knows how to shave his own head, though in regard to this he will generally be helped by his friends. But since the introduction of the safety razor, the art of shaving has greatly been simplified (Plate 18).

The Brotherhood is a community of men pursuing one common object, and the spirit of mutual help and service is everywhere evident in its life. Democracy is also made, as was already stated, one of the principles governing this social body.

SEWING AND MOXA-BURNING PLATE 17

SHAVING PLATE 18

Each monk, therefore, endeavours, on the one hand, to give others the least trouble for his own sake, while on the other he will do his utmost to do the most good he can for the general welfare of the community. This is known technically as "accumulating a stock of merit." It is natural that those who have successfully graduated from the Zendo life are some of the most efficiently trained and the most thoroughly equipped members of society.

To do service does not always mean to do something for others. If it is done with the thought of a reward or without the sense of gratitude and humility, it is not at all service, it is a deed of mean commercialism. The Zen monk ought to be above that. A life of service is closely related to that of humility and gratitude.

In the use of the materials, natural or artificial, which are the common possessions of the Brotherhood, the monks are taught to be scrupulously careful about not wasting or abusing them. Water is everywhere obtainable in this part of the earth, especially in the mountain monastery; but they are strictly instructed not to use it too freely, that is, beyond absolute necessity. An attendant monk to a Zen master was one day told to change water in the wash-basin as it had stood too long in it. The attendant carelessly threw it out on the ground. The master was indignant and said, "Don't you know how to make it work usefully?" The monk confessed ignorance, whereupon the master advised him to pour the water around the root of a tree which was evidently in need of moisture (Plate 19).

I said "usefully," but the correct rendering is "livingly," and there is in it a note peculiar to Zen. "To make the living use of a thing" and not "to make the dead use of it," means, economically speaking, to develop its efficiency to the highest possible degree in consideration of circumstances. But the Zen point of view is not to look at the matter economically or

D.T. SUZUKI

WASHING PLATE 19

dynamically: rather, if I could say so, "livingly" or "creatively." Merit, virtue, benefit, service, and other terms belonging to this category are conventionally religious. The way Zen handles so-called truths is satisfyingly fresh and stimulating; and there is at the same time a certain reverential attitude towards nature and her resources. In this machine age I have a strong desire to see this feeling of reverence towards nature restored and also the "living" use of things generally more properly appreciated by us.

This attitude of reverence towards nature, together with the idea that a man should not eat his meal unless he had something accomplished for the community to which he belongs, forms the foundation of the Zendo life. While the monk's mind is intensely occupied with the solving of the koan, which is more or less inevitably on the intellectual plane, he is liable to pay not so much attention to the social and practical aspect of his life. The doctrine of Emptiness (Śūnyatā), as we have seen elsewhere, tends to divert the thought of the Buddhist away from the world of particulars, though this is never the case with those who have truly grasped the doctrine. The two wings of the Buddhist life, therefore, are to be kept well balanced in power and activity, inasmuch as the monk is to develop this side of his life as a good student of Zen.

Modern life seems to recede further and further away from nature, and closely connected with this fact we seem to be losing the feeling of reverence towards nature. It is probably inevitable when science and machinery, capitalism and materialism go hand in hand—so far in a most remarkably successful manner. Mysticism, which is the life of religion in whatever sense we understand it, has come to be relegated altogether to the background. Without a certain amount of mysticism there is no appreciation for the feeling of reverence, and, along with it, for the spiritual significance of humility. Science and scientific technique have done a great deal for humanity; but as far as our really spiritual welfare is concerned we have not made any advance over that attained by our forefathers. In fact we are suffering at present the worst kind of unrest all over the world. The question is thus how to get us back to the appreciation of the Incomprehensible (acintya). This is no doubt the gravest and most fundamental of all the problems that are harassing people of modern times.

To come back to Zen. Ying, of Ting-shan seeing his head-monk washing his clothes, asked him: "What are you doing?" The monk held up the clothes. The master said: "What kind of clothes are those you are washing?" The monk answered, "I spent some money for them while at Fu-chou." The master told the overseer of the monastery to degrade the rank of this monk.

In the Zendo life a monk cannot even have his own laundry thoughtlessly done!

Shi, of Yang-shan, was washing his robe when Tan yuan came along and asked: "Where is your thought at this very moment?" Shi at once retorted: "At this very moment what thought do you want me to have?"

In Mahayana Buddhism various saints are worshipped. The bath room has a shrine dedicated to a Bodhisattva called Bhadrapāla, to whom the monks pay their respect before they take a bath. (Plate 20). Anciently, it is said that this Bodhisattva had his satori when he was about to bathe, and that the Buddha gave him this certificate: "The mysterious feeling of touch which you have now illuminatingly testified entitles you to the stage of Bodhisattvahood." This is one of the one hundred "cases" commented on by Hsüeh-t'ou (Seccho) in his Pi-yen Chi (Hekiganshu) His comment in verse reads when freely translated:

> "At last here is one who has successfully attained to the state of Emptiness;
> Stretching his legs in full length, he can now peacefully sleep on his long couch:
> But if you say that he has understood something to be discriminated as 'perfectly thoroughgoing,' I'll declare you to be still dreaming;
> However much you are washed in perfumed water your face remains forever bespotted, so long as your mind is not free from discrimination."

The monks are thus requested to wash off all the dirt of conceptualism as they are engaged in their daily work. But one may ask, "Where does this dirt come from, when we are told all the time by Mahayanists that we are from the first thoroughly clean and there are no defilements anywhere in us? Why then this constant bathing?" A master gives this answer: "Even the idea of cleanliness is to be done away with." Another master has: "Just a dip, and no why."

The following episode is of a different trend. Nan-ch'üan happened to pass by the bath-room, and seeing the monk attending to it said to him: "What are you doing?"
Monk: "I am heating the bath-water."
ch'üan: "Don't forget, when ready, to give a bath to the bull."
The monk said, "No, master," and towards the evening he came up to the Abbot's quarters.
ch'üan asked: "What are you doing here?"
Monk: "I want to get the bull and give him a bath."

BATH-ROOM PLATE 20

ch'üan: "Have you got a tether?"

The monk failed to answer. When Chao-chou came up to see Nan-ch'üan, the latter told Chou about this incident. Chao-chou said: "I know what answer to make." Whereupon Nan-ch'üan repeated: "Have you got a tether?" Chao-chou stepped forward and straightway took hold of ch'üan's nose and gave it a hard pull. ch'üan said: "It is quite proper, but how rough you are!"

To give another episode in connection with bathing. Tsan, of Ku-ling, came back, after some time of the Zen peregrination, to his own temple where he was ordained. His old master while taking a bath told him to scrub his back. Gently stroking the back of his old master who had yet no knowledge of Zen, Tsan said: "What a fine Buddha-hall! But there is no Buddha enshrined here." The master was angry at this remark and said: "O this lunatic, how could you be so rude?" Tsan made another remark: "Though there is yet no Buddha enshrined here, he knows just the same how to emit his rays."

The monks take their turn to be the bath-boy whose work in the bath-room is to scrub the back of the bather. As the back is hard to be thoroughly washed by oneself, the bath-houses in Japan are generally provided with back-washers who are ready to serve you for a few extra sen. When a monk is helped by his brother in this capacity, he folds his hands before him, expressive of his grateful acknowledgment of the service.

As we read in the bath-room regulations attached to this book, the material used for heating the bath-water is the dead leaves and other refuse gathered in the monastery yards.

Not to let your left hand know what your right hand does—this is known in the Zendo life as practising "secret virtue." It is also the spirit of service. Secret virtue is the deed done for its own sake, not looking for any form of compensation anywhere, neither in heaven nor on earth. The trouble with our social life is that we are always seeking for a reward, and more frequently for one enormously out of proportion to the merit of the deed itself. When this is not forthcoming, we are dissatisfied, and this dissatisfaction causes all sorts of trouble in our daily walk of life.

Human life is not always governed by economic principles: there is something more in it, and the peace and happiness we all are seeking is attained only when this "something more" is understood. It is most unfortunate that our modem life is systematically moving away from this thought, in fact deliberately trying to stifle the inner voice.

Buddhist teachers, therefore, earnestly urge to make us grasp the doctrine of Śūnyatā not only philosophically but in the most practical way. Unless this is done, the practice of secret virtue will be something artificial and, therefore, hypocritical.

How do we understand the doctrine? Ying-an T'an-hua, of T'ien t'ung, gives the following sermon: "Students of Zen should by all means avoid wrong applications of mind. To attain enlightenment or to see into one's own inner nature—this is a wrong application of mind; to attain Buddhahood or to become a master—this is a wrong application of mind; to recite the Sūtras or to discourse on the philosophy—this is a wrong application of mind; walking, staying, sitting, and lying—this is a wrong application of mind; putting on the dress and taking meals—this is a wrong application of mind; to attend to the calls of nature—this is a wrong application of mind; in fact, every movement you make, whether turning this way or that, or whether walking on this side or that—all this is a wrong application of mind. Kuei-tsung has never given you a discourse on the Dharma. Why? Because 'when one word passes in through the gate of the government office, even nine bulls are unable to get it out.'"

What is the ultimate signification of such a discourse as this? From the so-called common-sense point of view it looks like sheer nonsense. If we, following the literal meaning of the sermon, try to avoid "wrong applications of mind," where do we finally land? This very trying to follow the master—is this not also a wrong application of mind? He evidently teaches us not to awaken a thought, but to realise a state of acittatā, "no-mind-ness"; but this is again a faulty attitude of mind. A monk asked Yün-mên: "Is there any fault when not one thought is raised, or not?" Mên answered: "Mt. Sumeru!" If so, what is required of us to do in this impasse? Everything is taken away from us; the earth itself fails to support us. But this is the very situation into which all Zen masters contrive to drive us. A light flashes out of the darkness when the latter reaches its limits. Then we realise the truth of the following dialogue:

A monk asked Ch'e, of Shih-mên; "How shall we make an advance when no thoughts are cherished of anything?" The master's reply was: "The wooden man sits on the loom and the stone-man at night throws in the shuttle."

When this is understood, Śūnyatā becomes facts of our daily life, and the practice of secret virtue is no more Pharisaism. Any work, however offensive or repulsive in the ordinary sense, ceases to be so and is willingly undertaken.

Cleaning the lavatory, for instance, especially the one constructed in primitive style, is generally relegated to people whose profession is to do that kind of work. In the monastery, however, monks are disciplined to take up whatever work that is assigned to them without a murmur and to do it in the best possible manner. Apart from its moral or social value, this attitude of mind is cultivated, as we have already seen, from the point of view which may be called specifically Zen or Mahayanistic. The Christian idea of attending on unfortunate patients suffering from disgusting diseases, which is specially considered by the Christians to be pious or meritorious, shows a great similarity to the Buddhist motive. The thought at the back of the deed admits of variations, but the same feeling which may be called religious underlies here both the Christian and the Buddhist mind.

Ucchushma is the name of the god enshrined at the lavatory, who is supposed to swallow up all the impurities discoverable here. His business does not seem to be a very pleasant one; but as long as we are not beings thoroughly purgated of impurities inside as well as outside, there must be some who will take care of them; and this one no doubt is he who has reached the state of mind to which no "wrong applications" are possible (Plate 21).

Footnote

1. These recitations with many others are given, more literally rendered, towards the end of this book.

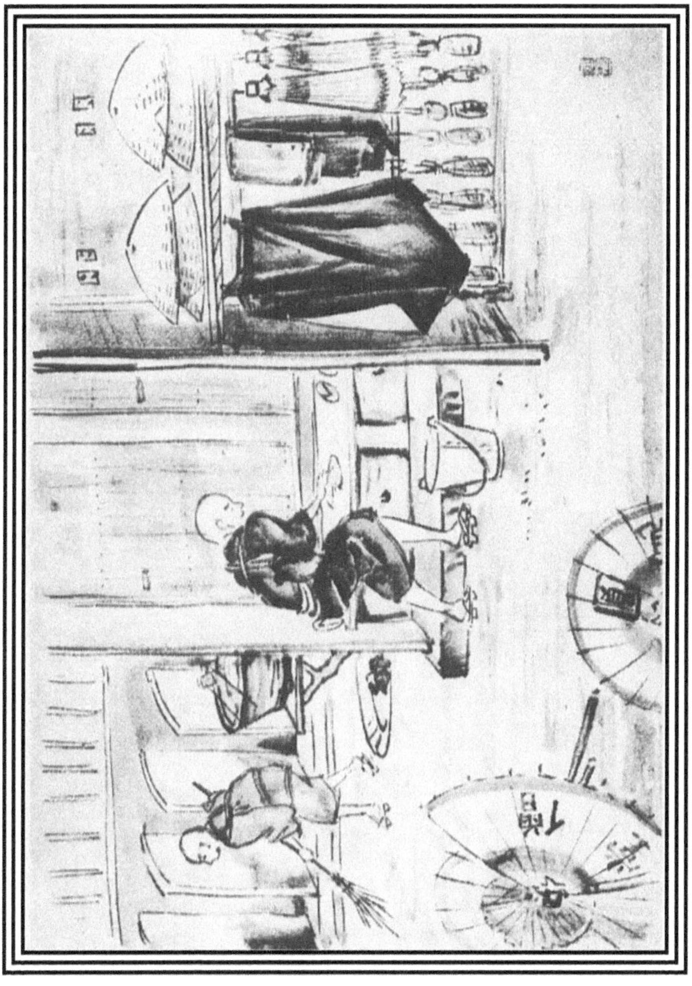

WORK OF SERVICE PLATE 21

LIFE OF PRAYER & GRATITUDE

THE LIFE OF prayer begins with confession; for prayer, in whatever sense it may be taken, is the expression of an earnest desire which is raised when the devotee feels something lacking in himself and seeks to complete himself either through an outside power or by digging deeper into his own being; and the confession consists in frankly recognising this fact which is in some cases felt as sinfulness. In Buddhist terminology, this means to grow conscious of the heaviness of one's own karma-hindrances which have been raised in the past by means of body, mouth, and mind. When the devotee is innerly impelled to become conscious of this, he prays. He may not have any definitive knowledge as regards the objective body to which his prayer is offered. This knowledge is not generally essential, because his prayer is the uncontrollable outburst of an intensely intimate desire. In Zen Buddhism prayers are offered to all the Buddhas and Bodhisattvas of the past, present, and future in the ten quarters and also to Mahāprajñapāramitā.

The confession formula is:

"All the evil deeds I have committed in the past are
due to greed, anger, and folly cherished since the
time beyond calculation,
And have been produced by means of my body,
mouth, and mind—
All these I now confess without reservation."

D.T. SUZUKI

With Zen Buddhists prayer is more in the form of self-reflection and vow or determined will than asking for an outside help in the execution of desires. The following is what is known as "the Bodhisattva's Vow and Deed":

"When I reflect upon the true character of all things I perceive that it is mysteriously expressive of the virtue of the Tathāgata and that the entire universe down to its smallest particles is a ray issuing from him in the most incomprehensible manner. For this reason the ancient masters have cherished a kindly and reverential attitude towards all beings inclusive of birds and beasts. In all the foods and clothes wherewith our body is kept warm and nourished through the twelve divisions of the day we recognise the flesh and blood of our masters; for even these inanimate objects reflect their love and compassion, for which we all feel the deep sense of reverence and gratitude. This being the case, we ought to think most tenderly and kindly towards those who are not sufficiently endowed with intelligence. Even when enemies vilify us or torment us in one way or another, let us consider them Bodhisattvas in disguise, whose loving hearts endeavour by this means to efface the effects of all our evil deeds and thoughts which we have been constantly committing because of our egotism and prejudiced views since the immeasurable past. Let us thus thinking cultivate the virtue of humility in words and deeds and raise with single-mindedness thoughts of devotion. The very moment when thus pure faith is awakened from the depths of our being, a lotus of enlightenment will open up in bloom. Each lotus flower carries a Buddha in it, and wherever there is the Buddha, there is a pure land in full array, and its glory will follow every step of ours. May this way of feeling be shared by all sentient beings and they together with us equally attain to the realisation of Sarvajñata!"

Ta-hui's prayer which is recited daily in the Zen monastery

may be said to sum up all that is stirred in the heart of the monk:

"My only prayer is to be firm in my determination to pursue the study of Truth, so that I may not feel weary however long I have to apply myself to it; to be light and easy in the four parts of my body; to be strong and undismayed in body and mind, to be free from illnesses, and to drive out both depressed feelings and light heartedness; to escape every form of calamity, misfortune, evil influence, and obstruction, so that I may instantly enter upon the right way and not be led astray into the path of evil; to efface all the evil passions, to make grow the Prajñā, to have an immediate enlightenment on the matter that most concerns me, and thereby to continue the spiritual life of the Buddhas, and further to help all sentient beings, to cross the ocean of birth and death, whereby I may requite all that I owe to the loving thoughts of the Buddhas and Patriarchs. My further prayer is not to be too ill, or to be too suffering at the time of my departure, to know its coming before hand, say, seven days ahead, so that my thoughts may dwell peacefully and properly on Truth; abandoning this body, unattached to any tie at the last moment, to be reborn without delay in the land of the Buddhas, and seeing them face to face to receive from them the final testimony of supreme enlightenment, and thereby enabled to divide myself infinitely in the Dharmadhātu to help universally all sentient beings in their fording the ocean of birth and death. These prayers are offered to all the Buddhas and Bodhisattva Mahāsattvas of the past, present, and future in the ten quarters, and to Mahāprajñapāramitā."

Besides these prayers, the monk recites the "Inscriptions on the Right-hand Side of the Seat" written by Chung-fêng the National Teacher:

"The Bhikshus in these latter days resemble in form those homeless ones but at heart have no feelings of shame and remorse.

"Their bodies are covered with the priestly robe but their minds are tainted with worldly defilements.

"They recite with their mouths the sacred scriptures, but they harbour in their minds greed and lust.

"During the day they are addicted to the pursuit of fame and wealth, while at night they are drunk with impure attachments.

"Outwardly they observe the moral precepts, whereas inwardly they are secret violators of the rules.

"Forever busy with worldly affairs, they are neglectful of disciplining themselves for deliverance.

"They are devoted so much to the cherishing of idle thoughts that they have already thrown away right knowledge.

"1. Have the desire for Truth firmly set up in order to be able to see into your own nature.

"2. Cherish deep doubt in regard to the koan you have and be as if biting at an iron ball.

"3. Keeping up your erect posture on the seat, never lie down in bed.

"4. Cultivate the sense of humility and remorse by reading books and sayings left by the Buddha and the Patriarchs.

"5. Keeping the body pure in accordance with the Precepts, never get it tainted, and the same is to be said of the mind.

"6. Behave yourselves on all occasions with quiet dignity and be in no circumstances rash and boisterous.

"7. Talk softly and in a low tone, do not be given up to idle jokings.

"8. There may be people who do not believe you, but do not let them deride you.

"9. Lie always ready to use your dusters and brooms in order to keep the monastery buildings and courts free from dust.
"10. Untiringly pursuing the course of Truth, never be addicted to excessive eating and drinking.

"Birth and death is the grave event,
Every moment of this life is to be begrudged,
Impermanency will be here too soon,
Time waits for no one.
"A rare event it is to be born as human beings, And we are now born as such;
It is not easy to be able to listen to the Buddha's teaching, And we have now listened to it.
"This being so, if we do not attain emancipation in this life, In what life do we expect to emancipate ourselves?"

Besides these prayers and admonitions, the Sūtras are also daily recited in the early morning and in the afternoon. In Japanese and Chinese Buddhism sutra-reading performs a double function; primarily as getting in touch with the thought of the founder, and secondarily as creating spiritual merit. The first may better be called sutra-study whereas the latter is properly sutra-reading or reciting, for the object is just to recite it, not necessarily accompanied by an intellectual understanding of its content. The recitation itself is regarded as meritorious as it is so stated in the Sūtras. Not only reciting or reading but copying is also merit-producing. The sutra reading in the Buddhist monasteries can thus be reckoned as a sort of prayer. The reading, even when its full meaning is not grasped, detaches one's mind from worldly concerns and self-centered interests. Though negative, the merit herewith gained tends to direct the mind towards the attainment of Sarvajñatā. The sutra-reading is also an expression of gratitude towards one's teachers, ancestors, and other beings generally. To be grateful in Buddhism means that Sarvajñatā has gained so much towards its realisation in the world. In this feeling there is nothing personal, that is, egotistic. The monks, therefore, in their daily exercises which consist in sutra-reading, prayer-recitation, incense-offering, bowing, and so on, express their appreciation of what the Buddhas, Bodhisattvas, patriarchs, teachers, and other personages have done for the Buddhist cause.

The Sūtras most commonly used in the Zen monastery are (1) The Prajñāpāramitā-hṛdaya-sūtra, known as Shin-gyō, (2) The Samantamukha-parivarta known as Kwannon-gyō, which forms a chapter of the Pundarīka Sūtra, and (3) The Vajracchedikā Sūtra or Kongō kyō in Japanese. Of these three, the Shingyō being the simplest is recited almost on all occasions. Besides these Chinese translations, the original Sanskrit texts in Chinese transliteration which is pronounced in the Japanese way are also used; they belong more or less to the Dhārani class of Buddhist literature and are altogether unintelligible, even when they are translated.

On some special occasions the Mahā-prajñā-pāramitā Sūtras in six hundred fascicules are read in the way known as ten-doku (chuan-tu in Chinese). Ten-doku means "to read revolving." As the Sūtras are of such a bulk, they cannot be finished within a prescribed period. The six hundred volumes are divided among the monks and each monk reads two or three pages in the beginning and at the end of each volume while the middle part is read by turning over the entire volume for a few times; hence the phrase "read by revolving." Each volume consisting of one long sheet of strong paper is folded up to so many folios, and when the monks read them "by revolving" the Sūtras look as if they were so many long narrow pieces of yellow cloth flying in the air. (Plate 22.) And especially because they recite them at the top of their voices, the whole scene is quite a lively one. The reading of the Sūtras is full of spiritual benefits not only for readers themselves but for all to whom the merit is dedicated. The first three early mornings of the New Year are devoted to this ceremony at all the Zen monasteries, when not only the welfare of the nation but the peace of the entire world is most earnestly prayed for.

An old lady once sent a messenger with money to Chao-chou, requesting him to "revolve" the whole Tripitaka. Chao-chou came down from his seat, and, walking around the chair once, said: "The revolving is finished. The messenger went back to the old lady and reported the proceeding as it happened. The old lady said: "I asked him to 'revolve' the entire Tripitaka but his 'revolving' covers only a half of the Tripitaka.

On this, Ta-hui, one of the great Zen masters of Sung, commented: "Some ask, 'What is the other half?' others say, 'Make another round'; or 'Snap your fingers'; still others say, 'Give a cough'; or 'Utter a kwatz!' or 'Clap the hands!' Those who make these remarks do not know what shame means. As regards 'the other half,' do never make such a remark as this: 'Make another round'! Even when hundreds of thousands of kotis of rounds are made, they are, from the point of view of the old lady, no more than a half Tripitaka. Even when Mount Sumeru is gone round for hundreds of thousands of kotis of times, they are, from the point of view of the old lady, no more than a half Tripitaka. Even when the great Zen masters of the whole empire walk round the mountain for hundreds of

THE REVOLVING OF THE PRAJNAPARAMITA SUTRA PLATE 22

thousands of kotis of times, they are, from the point of view of the old lady, no more than a half Tripitaka. Even when all the mountains and rivers and the great earth and everything that makes up this universe of multiplicities, including every plant and every blade of grass, each endowed with a long broad tongue, unanimously revolve the Tripitaka from this day on to the end of time, they are, from the point of view of the old lady, no more than a half Tripitaka."

Ta-hui remained silent for a while and continued:

"'The beautiful pair of ducks, embroidered in the finest style, is there for you to see as much as you like;
But take care not to deliver up the gold needle that did the work!'"

After these references, another Zen master gave his own idea saying: "The old lady claims that Chao-chou has only finished revolving a half of the Tripitaka. This is replacing the genuine by the spurious. The only thing that was needed at the time to say was this: Why not take the whole thing in even before Chao-chou started to walk round the chair?"

How the hungry ghosts came to find their place in the scheme of the Zen conception of the world is a subject of special research in the institutional history of Zen in China. Zen in its pure form has the tendency to become acosmistic, but in its "affirmative aspect" it accepts everything that is going on in the world of multiplicities. Even all the polytheistic gods including denizens of the air, of the earth, and of the heavens, and any other beings, who are living only in the realm of superstitional and traditional beliefs, are indiscriminately taken into the system of Zen. Each of them is permitted to have his or her place in Zen according to values given by the popular religions; and this is the reason why Zen has come to harbour so much of what I should call the Chinese Shingon element.

The Dhāraṇī-sutras are recited; ancestors are worshipped; the prosperity of the ruling powers of the time is prayed for,—although "to whom!" is the question still to be settled; the protection of the local gods is earnestly sought after; all the rituals in connection with the "departed spirits" are strictly observed; and all forms of exorcism are to a certain extent also practised. The Feeding of the Hungry Ghosts (segaki), which is observed at least twice a year during the Higan Season ("other shore") is thus one of the excrescences added from the outside; but at the same time the idea of a communion may be said to be noticed here, which is recognised to exist between all living beings and those who are supposed to have passed away. The form is to feed the hungry ghosts, but, as we can glean from the prayer-formula, the feeding is in reality sharing food, participating in the same staff of life, which symbolises the idea of one grand community comprising all the spirits seen and unseen.

The hungry ghosts, preta in Sanskrit, find their place in the six paths (gati) of existence. They are departed spirits, but as they seem to be eternally desiring something to eat because they are hungry, they are known as "hungry ghosts." Perhaps they betoken the human desire to have, which never knows satiation. If all the greed in the world expressing itself in infinite varieties of form is appeased by the performance of the Segaki ritual, the Pure Land will in no time be an actuality here with us. We are all then hungry ghosts, though not necessarily departed spirits. By feeding the supposedly departed we are feeding ourselves; when they are filled we are filled; no real distinction is to be made between the dead and the living. The living so called are living on the dead, that is, the dead so called are living most lively in the living. Prayer is then for being abundantly fed with Enlightenment, and gratitude is for enjoying this opportunity of realising Enlightenment together with the "departed spirits."

A tablet dedicated to "all the departed spirits of the triple world" is set up at the centre of the altar. Flowers, candles, and incense, together with food, are as usual offered to it. The holy enclosure is protected by the banners bearing the names of the Tathāgatas, Bodhisattvas, Arhats, gods, demigods, and other non-human beings. They are supposed, thus invited, to be present at the ceremony and participating in the erection of the mystic effects over the unhappy denizens of Limbo (Plate 23).

When the dramatis personae-Buddhas, gods, and hungry ones-are invited, the Dhāraṇīs are read and a prayer is recited to this effect:

"It is desired that all the hungry ghosts inhabiting every corner of the worlds filling, the ten quarters come to this place and partake of the pure food offered to them. You be filled with it, and when you are fully satisfied, you come here, and see to it that all sentient beings in turn are fed by you. It is also desired that by virtue of this magic food you shall be delivered from the pain you are suffering and be born in the heavens and visit as you will all the Pure Lands in the ten quarters; that you come to cherish the desire for Enlightenment, practise the life of Enlightenment, and in the life to come attain Buddhahood. It is again desired that you protect us days and nights so as to let us attain without hindrances the object of our lives. Whatever merit that is productive of this deed of feeding the hungry ones-let it be dedicated to the universal realisation of the Supreme Enlightenment and let every sentient being come speedily to the attainment of Buddhahood. This prayer is offered to all the Buddhas and Bodhisattvas of the past, present, and future in all the ten quarters, and to Mahāprajñapāramitā."

In fact, this feeding of the hungry ghosts and other spiritual beings is practised daily at the meal time. Before the monks

THE FEEDING OF THE HUNGRY GHOSTS PLATE 23

begin to take up their bowls of rice, they pick out about seven grains of it called saba and offer them to those non-human beings. The idea is perhaps partly thanksgiving and partly sharing good things with others.

Do those departed ones really come and hover about us?

When Tao-wu had a feast prepared in commemoration of his late master Yüeh-shan, a monk asked: "Why do you have this feast for your late master? Does he really come to take it?" Said Tao-wu, "How is it that you monks have the feast prepared?"

When Tan-yuan set up a feast for Chu the National Teacher on his death-day, a monk asked, "Will the Teacher come, or not?"

Yuan said, "I have not yet attained the art of mind-reading."

"What is then the use of setting up the feast?"

"I don't wish to discontinue the doings of the world."

When a similar question asked of Jên of Pai-shui, he said, "Have another offering ready." Did the master take the questioner for one of the hungry ghosts?

These statements by the masters do not seem to be very illuminating from our worldly relative point of view. Let us see what they say at the time of their departure about their own destination. Or, when we observe the manner in which they take leave of their earthly existence, it is perhaps possible for us to gain something of an insight into the whereabouts of the departed.

On the twenty-fifth of December, P'u, of Ho-shan, said to his attendants: "When a master dies it is customary for his Zendo followers to put up a special meal for him; but in my opinion this is altogether unnecessary. When I am to die, let me have your offerings before and not after my departure." The monks thought he did not quit his joking even in his old days. They asked, "When will you pass away?"

"I pass away when you all have had your offerings made to me."

A curtain was set up in his bed-room, behind which he sat; all the ceremonial vessels were placed before him, the eulogies were read, and food was offered him in due reverence. P'u the master had a good appetite and consumed all the food offerings, showing no symptoms of an early departure. The ceremony continued for some days until everybody in the monastery, including his immediate disciples down to all the coolies, duly paid his respect to the master who was thus treated as one really passed away. On New Year's day all the ceremony in connection with a death came to an end. The master said to the monks, "The time is come; tomorrow when it ceases to snow I will go." On the following day the weather was fair, but it began to snow, and when this stopped he passed away, quietly sitting and with incense burning.

When Hsiu, of Cho-chou, was about to die, he had a bath, and afterwards ordered to have a cup of tea brought to him. When he finished the tea, the attendant proceeded to carry the tea tray away; but the master withdrew the tray and said; "Do you know where I am bound for?" "No, master, I do not know." Whereupon the master handed the tray over to the attendant-monk, saying, "Go on, you do not know where I am bound for." When the monk came back after putting away his tray, he saw the master already passed out.

When Jên, of Su-shan, was asked where he was bound for after his death, he said, "Lying on his back in the heather, his four limbs point to the sky."

Mo, of Wu-hsieh, before his death, had a bath and incense burned. Quietly sitting in his seat, he said to the monks: "The Dharmakāya remains forever perfectly serene, and yet shows that there are comings and goings; all the sages of the past come from the same source, and all the souls of the world return to the One. My being like a foam is now broken up; you have no reason to grieve over the fact. Do not needlessly put your nerves to task, but keep up your quiet thought. If you observe this injunction of mine, you are requiting me for all that I did for you; but if you go against my words, you are not to be known as my disciples." A monk came out and asked, "Where would you depart?" "No-where." "Why cannot I see this 'no where'?" "It is beyond your senses." This said, the master peacefully passed out.

The Zen master's end was not always so peaceful; sometimes there were some who struggled hard to drop this "begging bag". When Chen, of Ts'ui-yen, was at the point of death, he suffered terribly, rolling on the straw matting which was spread over the ground. Chê the attendant was in tears as a witness of this agonising scene and said to the master, "While yet strong, you made all kinds of defamatory remarks on the Buddha, on the Fathers; and what do we see now?" The master gazed for a while at the attendant and scolded, "You too make this remark?" He now got up, and assumed a crosslegged posture, and, ordering the attendant to burn incense, quietly gave up the ghost.[1]

Footnote

1. For another example like this, see my Zen Essays, III, p. 35.

LIFE OF MEDITATION

THE SECRET WORLD OF THE ZEN BUDDHIST MONK

Now WE COME to the central facts of the zendo life, which constitute the characteristic training given to the Zen monk. The term meditation does not quite express the idea prevailing here, and what it really means when it is used in connection with the life of the Zen monk will become intelligible as we go on with its description below. Before going further, let me acquaint you with the construction of the Zendo. The Meditation Hall (zendo in Japanese and ch'an-t'ang in Chinese), as it is built in Japan, is generally a rectangular building of variable size according to the number of monks to be accommodated. As this number however does not as a rule exceed one hundred, the size of the Zendo is to that extent limited. The one at Engakuji, Kamakura, which was reconstructed after the earthquake of 1923, measures about 36 feet by 65 feet, which can contain fifty or more monks.

It has two entrances. The front one is shown in the Plate 24 and the rear one in the Plate 25. The tablet at the top of the entrance (Plate 24) reads Shō-bō-gen Dō meaning "The Hall of the Eye of the Right Dharma", because the hall is intended for opening the Dharma-eye of the occupants who with it can see into the secrets of life and the world. The square board of wood which the monk is about to strike is used for various purposes: to call the monks to meals, lectures, services, etc., or to tell them that the meditation hour has begun or ended. The characters on the board read:

> "Birth and death is a grave event;
> How transient is life!
> Every minute is to be grudged,
> Time waits for nobody."

THE FRONT DOOR OF THE ZENDO PLATE 24

The shrine behind the half-opened door contains generally the image of Mañjuśrī, who represents Wisdom (Prajñā). The opening of the Dharma-eye means acquiring this Prajñā, and the Bodhisattva is the fit object of worship in the Meditation Hall.

The rear entrance (Plate 25) is used by the monks for their private purposes such as washing, going on errands, etc. Observe those foot-gears in perfect order. They are of the simplest kind, but very well taken care of; and when the monks leave them at the door to enter into the Hall, they see to it that the getas are not scattered about in confusion. The wooden tablet over the entrance contains the regulations of the Hall, a translation of which is given below.

The interior of the Hall is furnished with raised platforms called tan which runs along the longer sides of the Hall. The tan is about eight feet wide and about three feet high. At one end of the empty floor oblong in shape, which occupies the centre of the building between the tan, there stands the shrine for Mañjuśrī the Bodhisattva, which opens towards the front entrance. This centre floor is used for an exercise called kinhin (ching-hsing in Chinese), which consists in circulating in Indian file along the tan (Plate 26). This is practised at definite intervals during the meditation hours. This walking helps to keep the monks' minds from falling into a state of torpidity.

The tan has a tatami floor, and a space of one tatami, about three by six feet, is allowed to each monk. This little space is for each monk his "heaven and earth," for here he sleeps, sits, meditates, and does all other things permitted in the Hall. Whatever little belongings he has are kept at the window-end of the tan, where a low closet-like arrangement is provided along the whole length of the tan. The bedding is put away on the spacious shelf constructed overhead and concealed with a curtain (Plate 27).

THE REAR DOOR OF THE ZENDO PLATE 25

KINHIN (WALKING EXERCISE) PLATE 26

When the hour to sleep comes which is ordinarily about 9 p.m., the monks recite The Shingyō (Prajñāpāramitā-hṛdaya-sūtra) and bow three times to Mañjuśrī. They lie down in one row (Plate 28).

The jikijitsu (chih-jih in Chinese), who directs every movement of the monks in the Hall—the most important office in the Zendo, seeing them all quiet under the futon, offers his last incense to the Bodhisattva and puts away his keisaku ("staff of admonition," ching-ts'e in Chinese) (Plate 28). When this is all done, he himself goes under a scanty futon. The one who sits on the opposite tan is called tantō, meaning the "head of the tan". His office is nowadays more or less honorary.

The bedding given to each monk is one broad futon or quilt wadded with cotton-wool, which is about six feet square in size. He wraps himself in this only, even in the midst of the cold winter, and sleeps from 9 p.m. till about 3.30 in the morning. For the pillow he uses a pair of small cushions, each about two feet square, on which during the daytime he sits and keeps up his meditation. As soon as he wakes, the bedding is put up to the common shelf overhead (Plate 27). He then goes out from the rear door to what may be called a general wash-stand. The stand holds one big basin filled with fresh water and supplied with a number of small bamboo dippers. The dipper does not hold much water. This is purposive, for, according to Zen philosophy, as was stated before, it is an act of impiety to use the gifts of nature too lavishly or more than is actually needed (Plate 29).

When Hsüeh-fêng (Seppa), Yen-t'ou (Gantō) and Chin-shan (Kinzan) were travelling together on their Zen pilgrimage they lost their way in the mountains. It was growing dark and there was no monastery to ask for the night's lodging. At the time they happened to notice a green vegetable leaf flowing down along the stream. By this they naturally inferred

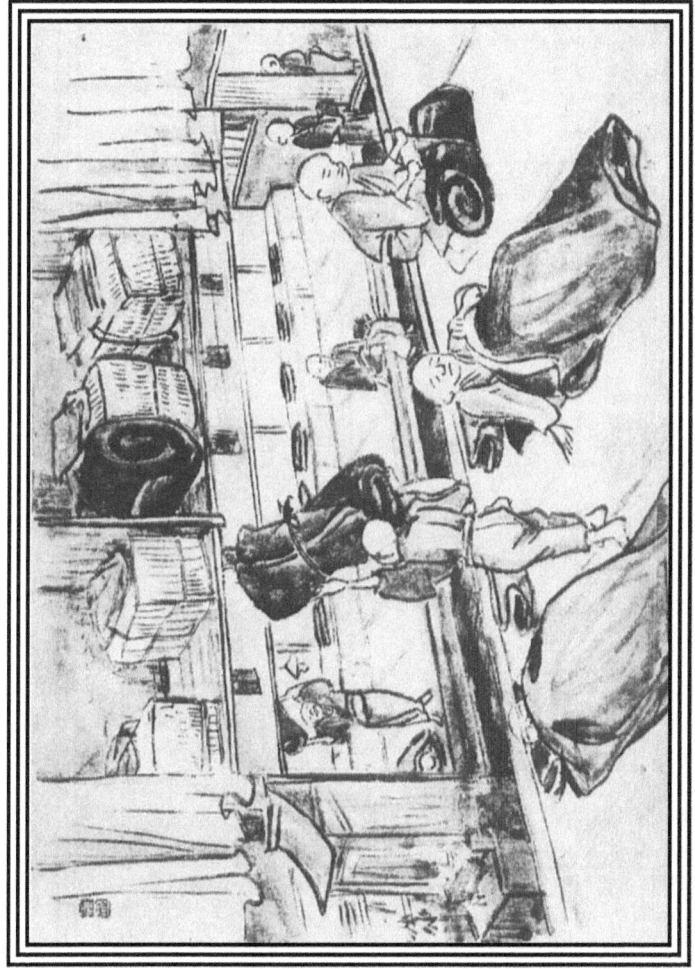

BEDDING PUT UP PLATE 27

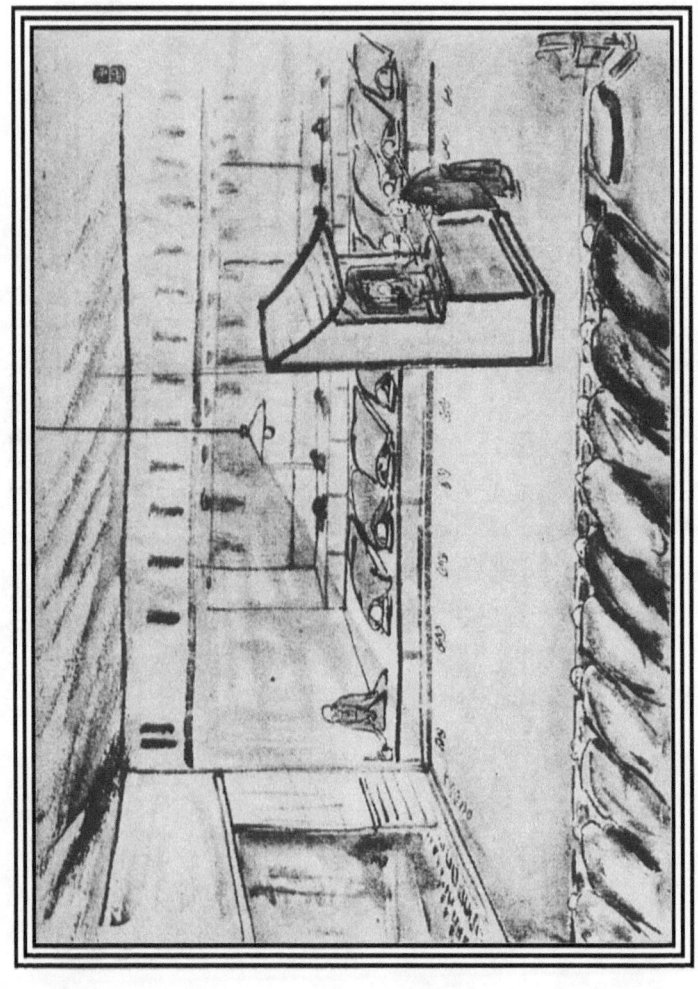

GOOD NIGHT TO THE HOLY MONK PLATE 28

MORNING WASH PLATE 29

that there was somebody living further up in the mountains. But one of the monk-pilgrims argued; "That is quite probable, but a man who does not mind letting go the precious vegetable leaf is not worth our consideration." Before he finished saying this, they saw a man with a long-handed hook, running down after the lost leaf. This may be an extreme case, but the legend beautifully illustrates what profound respect Zen feels towards the gifts of nature as well as the offerings of its pious devotees.

Humility, self-discipline, aspiration for the higher objects of life, etc. are at the bottom of the philosophy of asceticism. Asceticism is not always negativistic, nor does it issue from an unhealthy state of mind or from a perverted view of life generally. There is something positive, manly, and self-asserting behind the mask of a dry abnegation. To regard Zen as a form of asceticism and nothing more will be a grievous mistake. What Zen aims at is to reduce the claims of the body to a minimum in order to divert their course to a higher realm of activities. To torture the body is not its object, nor is it its object to gain merit and thereby to lay one's fortune in heaven. When a man sees higher values which he desires to realise in his own life not only for himself but for all his fellow-beings, he is always required to rise above the considerations of his merely physical welfare. The physical welfare of course is not to be altogether ignored so long as it is the vehicle for things higher than itself; but when it is given too much consideration it is bound to overstep the sphere properly belonging to it. This is one of the weaknesses inherent to human nature. Especially, when Zen sometimes appears to teach the gospel of antinomianism or latitudinarianism, it is well for Zen to emphasise the practice of self discipline in the life of the Meditation Hall. Even in trying to become an expert athlete, daily training involving a great deal of self-denial and asceticism is absolutely needed. If he indulges in any of his natural weaknesses, he is barred from entering into the arena. With those who aspire to denote themselves to the attainment and realisation of things of the highest value in life, how can they think of shrinking before a certain measure of discipline?

How much sleep is needed for a man to keep himself healthy, strong, and always capable for work is a great problem; it cannot be decided without considering various incidental circumstances besides his own hereditary constitution. But sleep seems to be something that permits much latitude, and discipline or habit can do much to reduce it to its lowest terms. Perhaps this is one of the reasons why the Buddha and many other great spiritual leaders severely denounce those indulgent in sleep. But from another point of view, sleep is indicative of peace and contentment; those who are always wakeful and look about with an unsteady gaze, or those who are startled at every little incident or mishap of life, and unable to fall asleep being so miserably nerve-racked, are those whose spirits are somehow maladjusted to the general scheme of the universe. In these modern times when environment by artificial means changes so rapidly, the very author of these changes finds it extremely difficult to adapt himself to them, and the result is the manifest growth of all kinds of neurotics. Is it not indeed refreshing then to find such examples as follows in the history of Zen?

Yen-t'ou Ch'üan-kuo, a great Zen master of late T'ang, seeing Su-shan (Sōzan) approach, fell soundly asleep. Shan came up to the master and stood by him, who, however, paid him no attention whatever. Shan gave one stroke to his chair. The master turned his head about and said, "What do you want?" Shan replied, "O master, have a good sleep!" So saying, he went off. The master laughed heartily: "I have for these thirty years fooled with so many horses, and today I find myself kicked down by an ass!"

While Tou-tzu I-ch'ing was in the monastery presided over by Yüan-t'ung Hsiu, he never came up before the master to make inquiries about Zen, but went on all the time dozing. The chief director appealed to the master, saying: "There is a monk in our Zendo who passes his time sleeping and doing nothing. He ought to be dealt with in accordance with the Regulations."

Hsiu: "Who is that?"

Director: "Brother I-ch'ing."

Hsiu: "Don't be hasty. Wait till I try him."

The master now took up his staff and went into the Hall. Seeing the said monk dozing, he struck the floor with his staff and scolded him, saying: "You cannot go on like this while consuming our rice."

Ch'ing: "What do you want me to do then, 0 master?"

Hsiu: "Why do you not study Zen?"

Ch'ing: "When a man's stomach is already filled up, to what fine meal are you going to treat me?"

Hsiu: "Unfortunately, there is one who does not fully endorse you."

Ch'ing: "What is the use of waiting for such endorsement?"

Hsiu: "Whom did you see before coming here?"

Ch'ing: "Fu-shan."

Hsiu: "I was wondering how you came to be so stubbornly self assuring."

So saying, the master took the hand of the sleepy monk, and smilingly left the Hall.

To reach this stage of understanding, however, is no easy task and will require an enormous amount of energy. Hence the following admonition by T'ui-yin in his Mirror for Zen Students: "Unless you reflect within and strive hard to realise the truth of it, the mere learning of so many Sūtras will be

THE SECRET WORLD OF THE ZEN BUDDHIST MONK

of no real avail to your spiritual welfare. It is like the birds chirruping in the springtime and the insects singing in the autumn nights—they all have no meaning beyond mere making noise. The sutra-reading ought not to be like this. When your study is not yet in complete tune with the truth, it may add to your reputation as a learned scholar or an eloquent speaker. However much you may excel in this, it is like painting your dirt-carrier in vermillion.

"The Buddhist monks ought not to be induced to study worldly or mere scholarly literature. It is like cutting a lump of clay with a sword: the clay itself does not gain anything in the way of its usefulness, while the sword is damaged beyond repairs. It is not a small matter—this abandoning the householder's life and becoming a monk. It is not to enjoy an easy, comfortable life, it is not to gain worldly glory or to amass wealth; it is for the sake of becoming free from the bondage of birth and death, it is to subjugate the tyranny of the passions; it is to continue the Prajñā-life of the Buddha; it is to deliver all beings from their transmigration in the triple world.

"The fire of transiency burns everything in the world, and the robbers of the passions are stealthily looking for every chance to take hold of your inner treasure. Those monks who are ever after wealth and reputation are worse off than the simple-minded peasants on the farm. Says the Buddha: 'Those who wearing my dress disparage the Tathāgata and amass all kinds of evil karma they are my enemies.'

"O monks, you are all sons of the Buddha; every thread of the dress you wear comes from the loom of the hardworking weaver, and every grain of rice you consume is indicative of the sweat of the farmer's brow. If your Prajñā-eye is not yet opened, what claim can you ever have on those precious gifts from your fellow-beings? Do you wish to know what animals they are who are covered with fur and carry a pair of horns on their heads? They are no other than those monks who accept shamelessly all the pious offerings from their devotees. Monks are not to eat while not hungry, they are not to wear anything more than they actually need. Instead of accepting from their pious-minded devotees fine raiment, a bowl of rice, or a hut, let monks wear a dress of red-hot steel, make a meal of molten metal, and live in a blazing kiln, if their hearts have not yet burned with the desire to save themselves as well as all beings from the despotism of birth-and-death, and if they are not straining all their spiritual energy towards the attainment of this end.

"Monks ought to behave like a grinding stone: Changsan comes to sharpen his knife, Li-szŭ comes to grind his axe, everybody and anybody who wants to have his metal improved in any way comes and makes use of the stone. Each time the stone is rubbed, it wears out, but it makes no complaint, nor does it boast of its usefulness. And those who come to it go home fully benefitted; some of them may not be quite appreciative of the stone; but the stone itself remains ever contented..."

This may be called non-resistance, or non-injury (ahiṃsā), but in Zen Buddhism it is known as cultivating "secret virtue," or practising "deeds of effortlessness" (anabhogacaryā).

What properly constitutes the study of Zen in the Zendo life is to study on the one hand the writings or sayings or in some cases the doings of the ancient masters and on the other to practise meditation. This practising is called in Japanese to do zazen, while the studying of the masters consists in attending the discourses given by the teacher of the Zendo known as Rōshi. Rōshi means literally "an old teacher," but in this case "old" means "venerable," and has no reference to the age of the master. The discoursing is technically called teishō or kōza. To give a teishō or kōza does not mean "lecturing on the textbook," it means to manifest the inner meaning of it. The master (Rōshi) does not explain anything, for he refuses to appeal to the intellect of his audience in his discourse; what he tries to do is rather to re-awaken in the minds of his monks the psychology of the ancient master that directed the course of the Zen interview in question.

This being the case, the monks whose Prajñā-eye still remains closed will not be any wiser after attending so many discourses given by the Rōshi.

The teishō is a solemn affair. When the hour approaches, the monk on duty strikes the board hung at the front entrance to the Zendo (Plate 24). The occupants make themselves ready by putting on a special cloth called kesa (kaṣāya in Sanskrit). When the drum or the bell is heard at the lecture hall, the monks filing themselves in due order leave the Zendo and walk in a most dignified manner to the room where the teishō takes place (Plate 30). When they finish sitting, the Rōshi comes out of his own quarters, accompanied by two attendant-monks (jisha).

As soon as he comes in, he walks towards the inner shrine where the Buddha is. A stick of incense is offered to him, to the founder of the monastery, to the succeeding abbots, and to the master of the Rōshi himself if he happens to be already dead. Each time an incense-offering is made, the Rōshi bows and prostrates himself three times on the floor. While this goes on, the monks recite three times a short Dhāraṇī-sutra dedicated to Kwannon Bosatsu (Avalo-kitesvara), and then once the spiritual admonition left by the founder of the monastery or by one of the great ancient masters, or the "Song of Meditation" (Zazen Wasan) by Hakuin. The recitation

D.T. SUZUKI

MONKS FILING UP PLATE 30

is punctuated by the mokugyo,[1] which is a large spherical wooden implement with the inside hollowed out and a fish pattern carved on the outside. It is struck with a short stick, one end of which is wrapped with a stuffed piece of leather. The sound helps to make the minds of the audience receptive for the ensuing discourse.

Now the Rōshi mounts the high chair facing the Buddha-shrine; one of the attendants sets a reading table before him, and the other a cup of tea (Plate 31). If the textbook is Lin-chi Lu ("Sayings of Rinzai"), the Rōshi will begin like this:

"Wō Jōji, Governor of this district, together with his officers asked the master (Rinzai) to take his seat. The Master mounted the platform and said: It was inevitable for me today not to accept the kindness of the Governor and others; I could not but yield to humanly feelings and find myself now in this pulpit. If I were to expound the great experience in accordance with the tradition of our ancient Fathers, there would absolutely be no need for opening my mouth at all; for here is no room for anybody to put in his feet. But, to respect the persistent request of the Governor, I will not today hide anything from you in my treatment of the truth of Zen. Are there some in this congregation, who, like great generals, dispose the army in battle array and hoist their banners for the good fight? I will testify to them before the congregation.

"A monk asked: 'What is the ultimate truth of Buddhism?'
"The Master gave a 'Kwatz!'
"The monk bowed.
"The Master said [sarcastically?] : 'The venerable brother can hold his point in controversy.'
"The monk asked: 'Whose tune do you play? and to what school do you belong?'
"The Master said: 'When I was at Huang-po, I asked him a question three times and was struck by him three times.'

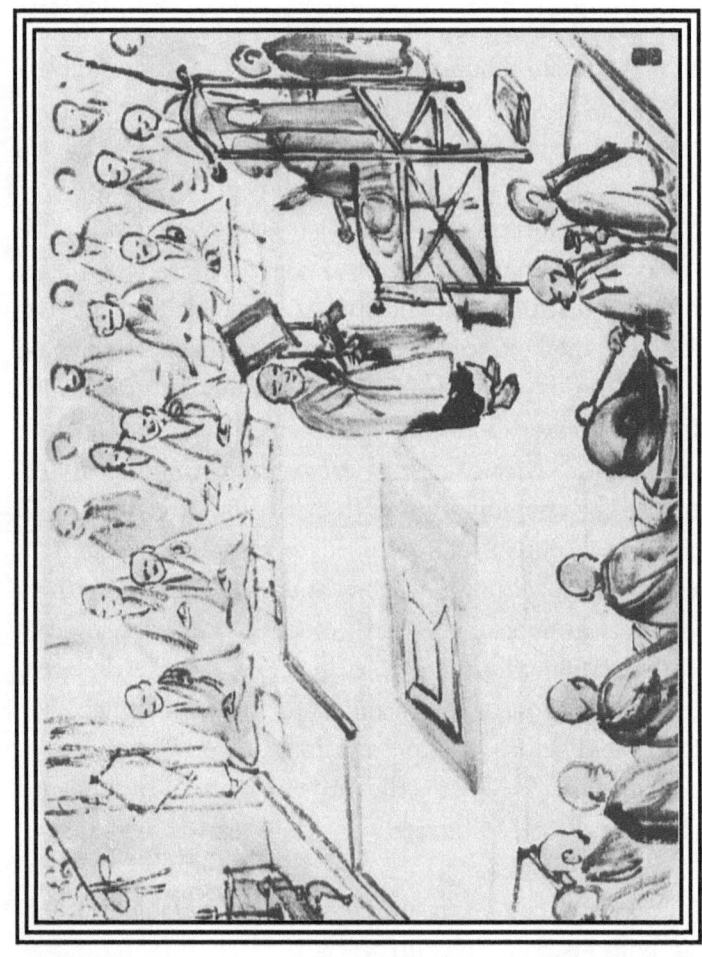

ROSHI READY FOR A KOZA PLATE 31

"The monk hesitated.

"Thereupon, the Master gave a 'Kwatz!' which was immediately followed by a blow and this: 'Impossible it is to fix nails onto vacuity of space.'

"A monk scholar came forward and asked: 'The Triple Vehicle and the Twelve Divisions-do they not all elucidate the Buddha nature?'

"The Master said: 'The rampantly-growing weeds have never yet been mown down.'

"The scholar said: 'The Buddha cannot be a trickster.'

"The Master pursued: 'Where is the Buddha?'

"The scholar remained silent.

"The Master said: 'There is no use of trying to confound me before the Governor. Be expeditious enough to give up your seat, forothers may be following.'

"The Master then continued: 'We are gathered here today for the sake of the one great event. Anyone wishing to ask me questions, come forward, don't delay. But the moment you try to say something, you slip off the board. Why is this so? Do you not know the Buddha say that the Dharma is beyond words, because it is not to be sought where causation rules? It is all due to your not having enough faith that I have appeared here today to make the matter worse confounded than ever. I am afraid that I have done enough to hinder the Governor together with his officers from having a clear insight into the Buddha-nature. It is best for me now to retire.'

"The Master now gave a 'Kwatz!' and said: 'O you, people of little faith! There is no end of work for you. I have kept you standing too long. Farewell.'"

In case of the text-book being the Hekigan Roku, the Rōshi's discourse will be something like this:[2]

"Preliminary Comment—When smoke is seen on the other side of the hill, one knows at once that there is a fire burning. When a pair of horns is noticed on the other side of the fence, one knows that a cow is grazing there. It is an everyday affair for a monk with any amount of intelligence to take in the whole situation even when he is allowed to have a glimpse only of its one corner. When all the streams are cut off, i.e., when the state of absolute Emptiness is realised, a man is capable of moving in every possible direction, beyond all the conceptual limitations imposed upon us by reason of our imagination and discrimination.[3] Whose behaviour can this be if such is ever attainable? Let us see what Hsueh-tau (Seccho), gives us as an instance of such a master."

"The Case—The Emperor Wu, of the Liang Dynasty, asked Bodhidharma the Great Teacher: 'What is the first principle of the Sacred Doctrine ?'

"Bodhidharma answered: 'In Vast Emptiness there is nothing to be designated "Sacred"'.

"The Emperor asked again: 'Who is he then who now confronts me?'

"Bodhidharma said: 'I know not.'

"The Emperor failed to grasp the meaning, and finally Bodhidharma crossed the River and went off to the Kingdom of Wei. Later, the Emperor asked Chih-kung (Shiko) about this interview with Bodhidharma. Said Chih-kung: "Do you know this man?' The Emperor confessed his ignorance, saying: 'I really do not know him.'

"Chih-kung said: 'He is a Kwannon Bosatsu attempting to transmit the seal of the Buddha-mind.'

"The Emperor was grieved and tried to hasten an envoy after Bodhidharma. But Chih-kung said: 'It is of no use for your Majesty to try to send for him. Even when all the people in this land run after him, he will never turn back.'

"The poetical comment—

"The sacred truth is Vast Emptiness itself,
And where can one point out its marks ?
'Who is he who confronts me?'
'I know not'—his answer this.
Thereby in the dark he crossed the River;
But what thorny brambles that have grown after him!
Pursued even by the entire populace of the land, there is no turning back for him.
For all the time to come we vainly think of him;
No, let us no more think of him;
A refreshing breeze sweeps all over the earth to its remotest ends.

"Seccho now turned his head, and, looking around him, said: 'Is there a patriarch among us here?' The answer came from himself: 'Yes, here he is. If so, let him come over here, for I want him to wash my feet.' "

When the koza is over which lasts about an hour, the entire audience recites the "Four Great Vows," and the monks go back in the same orderly manner as before to their own quarters. The Vows are:

"However innumerable sentient beings are, I vow to save them;
However inexhaustible the passions are, I vow to extinguish them;
However immeasurable the Dharmas are, I vow to study them;
However incomparable the Buddha-truth is, I vow to attain it."

The object of zazen or meditation in the life of the Zen monk is to open the Prajñā-eye. As we read in the Prajñā-pāramitā Sūtra, without the Prajñā all the other virtues are incapable of accomplishing anything, for they lack 'the eye which sees into the meaning of things generally'. The monk, therefore, must by all means have the scale cleared off by means of his koan, which is a kind of question given him for solution. When one koan is successfully solved, another is given until the master is thoroughly satisfied with the understanding of his monk. There is a large number of such questions available for the purpose. But in fact when one koan is grasped in a most penetrating fashion, all the remaining ones present no substantial hindrances to the final Zen realisation. The koan exercise is the most important feature in the Zendo life.

A special posture is recommended, though the koan exercise can be carried on in whatever work one may be engaged and in whatever bodily position one may assume; for Zen has nothing to do with the form the body may take, sitting or lying, walking or standing still. But for practical reasons the following posture is considered conducive to the acquirement of the mental attitude which is favourable to the Zen experience (Plate 32) :

When a man wishes to practise meditation, let him retire into a quiet room where he prepares a thickly wadded cushion for his seat, with his dress and belt loosely adjusted about his body. He then assumes his proper formal posture. That is to say, he sits with his legs fully crossed by placing the right foot over the left thigh and the left foot over the right thigh. Sometimes the half-cross-legged posture is permitted, in

MEDITATION POSTURE PLATE 32

which case simply let the left leg rest over the right thigh. Next, he places the right hand over the left leg with its palm up and over this rests the left hand, while the thumbs press against each other over the palm. He now raises the whole body slowly and quietly, moves it repeatedly to the left and to the right, backward and forward, until the proper seat and straight posture is assured. He will take care not to lean too much to one side, either left or right, forward or backward; his spinal column stands erect with his head, shoulders, back, and loins each properly supporting the others like a chaitya. But he is advised to be cautious not to sit too upright or rigidly, for he will then begin to feel uneasy before long. The main point for the sitter is to have his ears and shoulders, nose and navel stand to each other in one vertical plane, while his tongue rests against his upper palate and his lips and teeth are firmly closed. Let his eyes be slightly opened in order to avoid falling asleep. When meditation advances the wisdom of this practice will grow apparent. Great masters of meditation from of old have their eyes kept open. When the position is steadied and the breathing regular, the sitter may now assume a somewhat relaxed attitude. Let him not be concerned with ideas good or bad. Let him concentrate himself on the koan, which is to think the unthinkable by going beyond the realm of thought. When the exercise is kept up persistently for a sufficient space of time, disturbing thoughts will naturally cease to assert themselves and there will prevail a state of oneness, which is however not to be understood conceptually.

In the Zendo all the monks sit facing one another along the tan. The practice of the Soto School, however, is just the opposite: instead of facing one another the monks of one tan sit with their backs turned against those of the opposite tan. When they are not actually engaged in outdoor work, or when they are permitted to look after their personal affairs, they are invariably found sitting in meditation in their Zendo.

There is a special period generally once a month during the "stay-at-home" season, which is May-August and November-February. The period called "Great Sesshin" lasts one week. Sesshin means "to collect thoughts," and during this period the monks are exempt from work and practise zazen from early morning (3.30 a.m.) till evening (9.30 or 10 p.m.), except when they eat and when they attend the kōza which now takes place once every day.

Without doing what is known as sanzen, zazen does not bear fruit. Sanzen means the monk's seeing the master and presenting his views on the koan. Ordinarily, this takes place as a rule twice a day, but during the great sesshin the monks have to see the master at least four times a day. But if they have no special views to present for the master's examination it is not necessary for them to do sanzen. This kind of sanzen is called dokusan, individual or voluntary sanzen. At the sōsan, however, no monks are allowed to stay away from seeing the master (Plate 33). Sōsan means "general sanzen." This is enforced three times while the sesshin is going on.

When the bell rings at the master's quarters, those monks who have prepared an answer, go out each singly by the front door. The Zen interview with the master takes place in his own room. Before a monk invades the latter, he strikes the bell and announces his coming. (Plate 33). He may meet the one who preceded him and is now on his way back. He bows at the entrance to the room where the master sits quietly like a crouching lion and awaits the monk. Once in this room and all the preliminary bowings over, the monk is ready to behave himself in the way best expressive of his view. No conventionalism will restrain his giving the master a slap or a kick. On his part the master may strike the prejudiced monk and most violently chase him out of the room. The confusion thus ensuing may be heard even in

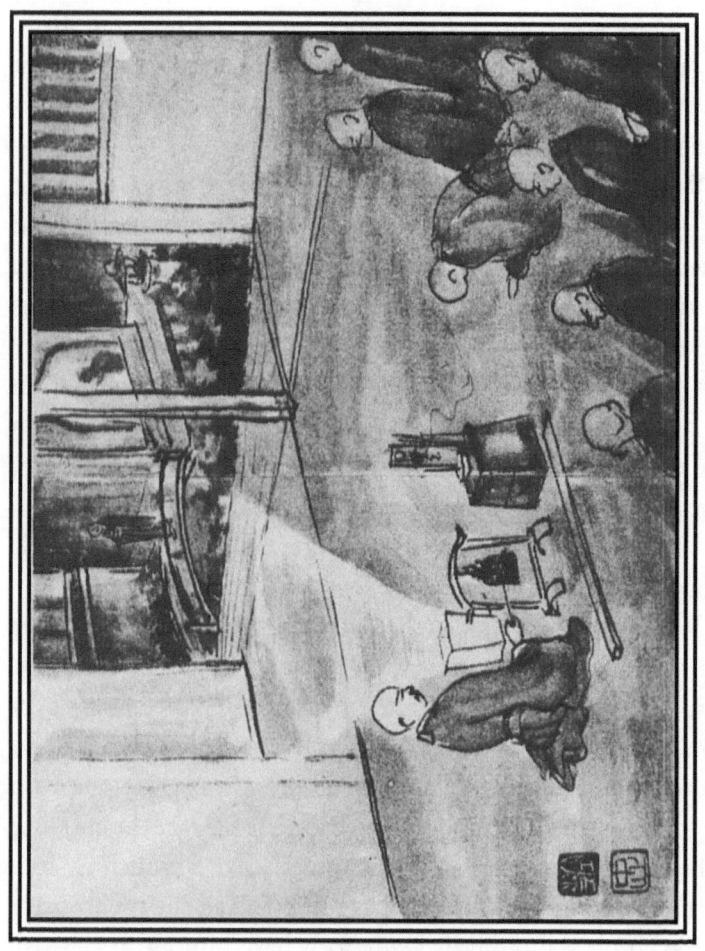

READY FOR A ZEN INTERVIEW PLATE 33

the waiting room where the monks congregate, each biding the time for his turn (Plate 34).

In the meantime another kind of confusion may be proceeding in the Zendo. On the occasion of sōsan, or when the senior monks deem the time maturing, they will urge those brother-monks to go to sanzen, who stay away too frequently from it. It is one of the most trying experiences in the life of a young monk to be thus urged by his seniors. He is not deliberately shunning the interview with the master; he really wants to see him and get his koan satisfactorily disposed of; he has almost exhausted all his energy in the endeavour to come to this happy conclusion. But he has now nothing to say; he knows no way to get out of the impasse; he stands at the end of a pole—no way to go ahead, and no way to beat a retreat; he feels, again, as if walking deeply enveloped in a dense fog. In the psychology of Zen this is the critical moment, and unless something desperate is not decided upon by the perplexed monk, there will be no further opening for him. To help him in this, his seniors will use physical force to pull him down from the tan, or to tear him away from the post or the door to which he clings with might and main. A scene of regular wrestling matches will be enacted in the midst of the quiet solemn atmosphere of the meditation hall (Plate 35).

That, in the breaking-through of the psychological crisis which is experienced in the study of Zen, an emotional excitement of the highest order is frequently needed, is quite evident. Zen is full of such instances, and the masters are never weary of advising their followers to exert their psychic energies to the utmost.

Suiwo was one of the great disciples of Hakuin. He had a monk from Ryūkū who wished to solve the koan of "One Hand." He stayed with the master for three years, but no enlightenment came over him. He was greatly disturbed

INTERVIEW WITH ROSHI PLATE 34

DEEDS OF THE UTMOST KINDNESS PLATE 35

because he could not possibly stay with his master beyond the period of three years. His disappointment knew no bounds. He could not think of going back with no new spiritual outlook to his native island which lies over beyond the south-western end of Japan. Suiwo comforted him saying, "Don't be grieved, but go back to your seat and devote the coming week exclusively to the mastery of the koan." When the week was over, the monk appeared before Suiwo with nothing to show to him. Said the master, "Never mind; but go on with your zazen for another week, and you will surely have an insight this time." The monk faithfully followed the advice. But at the end of the week he was the same old monk with no experience whatever. The master was not, however, discouraged, for he told him again to try for another week reciting examples of some ancient masters. The monk went back to his quarters with a renewed courage. The third week passed, but no result. He was then the most miserable man in the world. Utterly dejected in spirit and body, he came to the master for some means to help him out of the inextricable difficulties which were glaring at him. The master was apparently not yet at the end of his resources; he told the monk to try a sesshin of five days this time instead of seven.

The five days went on like the preceding seven days, and the monk was naturally almost at his last grasp. Beyond this, there was nothing left for him but to yield his breath, either out of despair or out of despondency. The master now said to him: "If you cannot come to any result after so many weeks of meditation, limit your time now to three days, apply yourself most intensely with all the psychic power there is in you to the solution of the koan, and if you still fail death is the only way now left to you." The monk made up his mind as was told by the master. On the third day sure enough a light dawned on him and he finally penetrated into the meaning of the "One

Hand." Perhaps the master was a happy man no less than the monk himself.

The Christian theologians may have their own doctrine to explain this kind of experience and also their own way of bringing it about. But psychologically the process is well known, and the Zen masters out of their own experience give advices purporting to create what may be called the Zen state of consciousness. The master Pan-jo (Hannya) has this for his monks: "When your mind is steadily and intensely and without interruptions on the koan, you will begin to be unconscious of your bodily existence, while the koan occupies the centre of your consciousness. At this stage, however, you have to be careful not to give up yourself to unconsciousness, for you are sometimes apt to go astray as in a dream and induce a state of insanity. Do never let your hold go off the koan, let the latter be present all the time in your consciousness. The time will come when together with the koan everything vanishes out of your mind including the mind itself. At this very instant, as when a bean pops out of the cold ashes, you realise that while Chang is drinking Li becomes tipsy."

Ku-mei Yu's (Kyozan Kobai Yu) advice is: "What is needed in the beginning of your exercise is to stir up your spunky spirits and be most resolutely determined to go on with your task. Summarily making a bundle of all you have hitherto understood or learned, together with your Buddhist knowledge, your literary accomplishments, and your clever manipulation of words, sweep it off once for all into the great ocean; and never think of it again. Gathering up eighty-four thousand thoughts into a seat, which enter into every hidden corner of your consciousness, squat on it, and strive to keep your koan all the time before your mind. Once lifted up before the mind, never let it slip off; try to see with all the persistence you find in yourself into the meaning of the koan given to you, and never once waver in your determination to get into the very bottom of the matter. Keep this up until a state of satori breaks upon your consciousness. Do not make a guess-work of your koan; do not search for its meaning in the literature you have learned; go straight at it without leaning on any kind of intermediary help; for it is in this way only that you can make for your own home..."

According to P'u-yen Tuan-an (Fugan Dangan), the following is the method to reach one's own final abode: "All things are reducible to the One, and where is this One reducible? Keep this koan in your mind and never allow yourself to think that quietude or a state of unconsciousness is the sine qua non in your koan exercise. When you feel confused in your mind so that your power of attention refuses to work its own way, do not try to gather it up again by means of a thought, but mustering your spirits keep up your koan by all means before you. Courage and determination are most in need of at this juncture.

"But if you still feel dull and confused and unable to bring the thought to a focus, get down from the tan and walk for a while somewhat briskly. After a while you will find yourself much refreshed; you will then come back on your cushion and continue your exercise. Suddenly there prevails a state of consciousness in which your koan rises on its own accord before the mind, asking for its own solution and refusing to vanish away from the centre of your attention. You do not then know whether you are walking or sitting, your 'spirit of inquiry' alone occupies the whole field. This is called the stage of passionlessness or egolessness, but this is not yet an ultimate state; another strong whipping is needed, and you must double the effort to see where after all the One is to be reduced.

"At this stage you do not feel any definite advance made in the 'lifting-up' of the koan. 'The spirit of inquiry' so intensely working out its own way, there is no conscious effort on your part to continue the koan exercise. After a while even this is swept away, and you attain a state of unconsciousness in which there is neither the koan nor the one who holds it. This is what is known as the stage of objectlessness. Is it a final one? No, by no means. Says an ancient master: 'Don't think the state of unconsciousness is the truth itself, for there is still another frontier-gate which is now to be broken through.'

"While you are in this state of mind, you happen to hear a sound or to see an object, and the whole thing comes to a sudden end; you have at last touched the ultimate reality. Nothing is left to you at this moment but to burst out into a loud laugh. You have accomplished a final turning and in very truth know that 'when the Kuai-chou cow grazes the herbage, the I-chou horse finds its stomach filled.'

From all these advices which are at the same time records of the experience lived through by the Zen masters, we can see what the koan exercise means and where the Zendo life leads us. The monks are not idling away their precious time in the monastery. They are trained here in a peculiar way to develop their moral and spiritual energies and also to see into the mysteries of their being. When all this is appraised in the proper light, we can appreciate the real significance of the Zendo life, which goes on in away so contrary to modern trends of thought and actual living.

While a great sesshin is going on, there is a general tension of nerves all around. Though the wisdom of such an institution is sometimes problematical there is no doubt about its doing immense good to those who have first entered upon the Zendo life. The development of the koan exercise is inevitably followed by the institution of the sesshin. However this may be, the nervous strain periodically experienced is a good practical discipline for all young men whether they are Zen followers or not.

That the so-called meditation practised in connection with the koan exercise is not the same mental training as is generally understood in the West, will now be plain to all who have studied the preceding pages. That is to say, to practise zazen is not the same as practising meditation. As so much psychic energy is concentrated on the "lifting-up" of the koan, the physical side of our existence also undergoes great pressure; and the result is that the muscles become cramped and the nerves too taut. To relieve the monk of this kind of discomfort, his shoulders are frequently slapped with a stick called keisaku, which means "staff of admonition." The staff is also used to prevent a monk from falling asleep while sitting in meditation. While the zazen hours are on, a monk with the keisaku stands at the end of either tan, keeping a close watch on his brother monks (Plate 36).

The monks who are desperate with their koans often quietly slip out of the Zendo and pass the night outdoors, sometimes on a flat rock which is found near the Zendo, or sometimes on the porch of a building, or in the cave which was probably once the favourite retreat of the founder of the monastery (Plate 37).

In the Zendo no books are allowed except when they are absolutely needed, for instance, when the monks have to look up a passage expressive of their understanding of a koan. This is required of them by the master when they successfully solve a koan. A book called Kuzōshi or Zenrin Kushū contains various kinds of passages relating to Zen. It is one of the vade-mecums to be carried along by all Zen students—monks and lay-disciples. This practice of regularly looking up the passages

THE SECRET WORLD OF THE ZEN BUDDHIST MONK

THE WARNING STAFF PLATE 36

culled from ancient literature helps the monks very much to become acquainted with the literary and cultural phase of the Zen life. In olden days, it was a part of the liberal education for the monks, who were taught to despise book learning and who thus came to be too one-sided and prejudicial of the ancient lore bequeathed by their predecessors. When they have to wade through the ō or some other books, they go out of the Zendo and turn their pages hurriedly under the dark light near the lavatory (Plate 38). In any event even today the Zen monks are unreasonably disposed against books and the culture based on their study. This is surely the outcome of their Zendo training.

Zen may sometimes go too far in its discouragement of the study of Buddhist literature or in its depreciation of scholarly attainment, but this discouragement or depreciation has been the traditional policy of its masters. There is no doubt that the policy, in spite of its sometimes untoward consequence, has imparted a refreshing atmosphere to the conventionalised Buddhist life.

A keeper of the Tripitaka once noticed a monk sitting quietly for some time in his library building. Asked the librarian: "Why don't you read the Sūtras?" "I don't know letters," was the monk's reply. "If so, why don't you ask people to teach you?" So advised, the monk stood up respectfully holding up his hands before his chest, and said: "Pray tell me what character this is." The librarian, failed to enlighten him.

Wang, one of the government officers, visited the monastery under Lin-chi (Rinzai). As they entered the grounds Wang asked,

"Do the monks here read the Sūtras?"
"No, they do not," replied Rinzai.
"Do they then study Zen?"
"No, they do not."
"If they neither read the Sūtras nor study Zen, what do

DEEPLY ABSORBED IN MEDITATION PLATE 37

MONKS LOOKING FOR ZEN PASSAGES PLATE 38

they do here?"

"They are all going to be made Buddhas and Fathers."

"Even precious particles of gold dust prove to be disastrous when they get into one's eyes. What do you say to that?"

"I thought you were a mere layman," was Rinzai's comment.

A monk came up to Yu of T'ien-kai, and asked, "I wish to read the Sūtras, and what would you advise me to do about it?" The master remarked, "Do you think a great merchant would bother himself about making a few cents?"

A monk asked Yeh-hsien, "Is it advisable to read the Sūtras, or not?" Said the master, "There are no byroads, no cross roads here; the mountains are all the year round fresh and green; east or west, in whichever direction you may have a fine walk." The monk said, "I wish to learn something more definite from you." "It is not the sun's fault if the blind cannot see their way," concluded the master.

P'ang, the great layman of Zen, once attended the lecture given by a Buddhist scholar on the Vajracchedikā. When the scholar began discoursing on the Prajñā philosophy of "no-ego and no-personality," P'ang queried, "If there is neither ego nor personality, who is lecturing now? And who is the audience?" The scholar made no reply, whereupon P'ang said, "Though I am a mere layman, I know a thing or two about the ultimate truth of the Buddhist teaching." Urged to express himself, he continued:

> "No-ego, and again no-personality,
> There is neither subject nor object;
> I advise you: Cease further lecturing,
> And seek the truth without any intermediary;
> In the Prajñā itself which is known as Vajra,
> There is not a particle of dust defiling it;
> From the beginning to the very last,
> The whole sutra is no more than words."

The koan exercises which are the prevailing method at present of mastering Zen involves many years of close application. Naturally, there are not many graduates of the Zendo life, and this is indeed in the very nature of Zen; for Zen is meant for the élite, for specially gifted minds, and not for the masses. This has been the case since olden days, but especially it is true in this modern age when democracy is the ruling spirit in all the departments of human life. Standardisation so called goes on everywhere, which means the levelling-down or the averaging-up of inequalities and "class distinctions." Unless aristocracy in one form or another is admitted and to a certain extent encouraged, the artistic impulses are suppressed and no religious geniuses will be forthcoming. Institutions like the Zendo are becoming anachronistic and obsolete; its tradition is wearing out, and the spirit that has been controlling the discipline of the monks for so many hundred years is no more holding itself against the onslaught of modernism. Of course, there are still monks and masters in the monasteries all over Japan, and yet how many of them are able effectively to respond to the spiritual needs of modern youth and to adjust themselves to the ever changing environment created by science and machine? When the vessels are broken, the contents too will be spilt out. The truth of Zen must somehow be preserved in the midst of the prosaic flatness and shallow sensationalism of present-day life.

The Zendo life is considered finished not only when the truth of Śūnyatā is intuitively grasped, but when this truth is demonstrated in every phase of practical life with its multitudinous trials, duties, and complications, and also when a great heart of Kamna (love) is awakened in the way rain falls on the unjust as well as on the just, or in the way Chao-chou's stone bridge is trodden on by all sorts of beings,-by horses, donkeys, tigers, jackals, tortoises, hares, human beings, etc.

This is the greatest accomplishment man can achieve on earth, and every one of us cannot be expected to be capable of this; but there is no harm in our doing the utmost to approach the ideal of Bodhisattvahood, if not in one life, then in lives to come through kotis of kalpas. When something of this ideal is firmly grasped, the monk takes leave of the Zendo (Plate 39) and begins his real life among his fellow-beings, as a member of the great community known as the world. As we observe in the picture, the whole Brotherhood comes out to see such a graduating senior monk off from the monastery gate. The scene is quite different now. When he first applied for admittance into the community, he was regarded almost as persona non grata, and all harsh treatment was accorded to him. But he has successfully buffetted the waves, ridden the storm finally to the harbour of safety, and he is ready for his mission among his fellow-beings which he will perform in whatever form he deems most expedient. Such ones are, indeed, to be also most enthusiastically greeted by the outside world.

Having been nourished among nature-mystics and born metaphysicians, Zen may seem to be lacking in religious feeling or in the emotional aspect of the religious life. At least as far as its literary expressions go, Zen abounds in allusions to objects of nature and statements indicative of philosophical aloofness.
"The birds fly high in the air, the fish swim and dance in the water."

SEEING OFF A SENIOR MONK PLATE 39

"The clouds are peacefully floating over the mountains, the stream is hurriedly running below the porch."

"The bamboos are growing thick, the pines are towering high, and how refreshingly green the mountains are!"

"Look at the steaming clouds about to leave the mountain-peaks, and listen to the murmuring stream which flows dancing over the rocks."

The moon, bright and serene, shines over the peaks after peaks; the wind blows rustling through branches of trees ten thousand years old." (Plate 40).

If I begin to cite such passages as these, there will be no end to them. Most Zen masters have passed their lives in the mountain monasteries, and it is natural for them to make references to the surrounding views when they are asked about Zen. Besides this fact, nature is to the Oriental mind something most intimate and appealing. She speaks her inmost yearnings directly to our hearts. In the waving of a blade of grass the intelligent eye detects a power transcending the vicissitudes of human life. The moon is not a mere heavenly body—an object of telescopic investigation or spectrum analysis; but in it there shines a light which makes us see into the eternity of things. Is this the imagination of the poet, or no more than the fantasy of a dreaming mind? Even so, there are many souls who perceive in this dream things of a very much higher value than so called scientific knowledge. I would loathe to see this type of mind wiped away before the on-coming tide of modern rationalism.

In Zen literature there is an expressive term called kafū or kyōgai. Kafū literally means "household air," or "house atmosphere;" or "family tradition." Kyōgai is "a sphere," or "a realm," that is, "an area enclosed within boundaries." Kyōgai and Kafū express practically the same idea: kyōgai as a more subjective and psychological connotation while kafū is historical

ZEN MONKS ON PILGRIMAGE PLATE 40

and may be conceived as a kind of atmosphere prevailing in a given community. In the history of Zen, questions frequently concern this "spiritual atmosphere" in which the master is moving, or the general psychological attitude or reaction characterising a Zen master as such. These questions amount to asking about the fundamental teaching of Zen, for when we know where the master's abode is, we know also where Zen finally purports to lead us. In the Sūtras, such words as gocara, vihara, or sthāna are used to denote the same conception. The following answers given by various masters as culled at random from the annals of Zen will help us to surmise where is the final destination of the Zendo life and of the koan exercise:

"The garden is terribly dry; have the spinach well watered."
"The moon is rising from the ocean and its rays reach far and wide."
"The blue sky and the broad daylight."
"The spring breeze is still blowing cold against my face; I wonder for whom is this brightly shining moonlight."
"Each time it is held up it is a new thing."
"I belong to one of the despised classes, whose forehead is broad."
"I am the standard of all the world."
"A simple meal of rice and soup."
"A silver bag of perfume behind the brocade screen makes the whole avenue odorous as it blows."
"With one bowl and one staff, I make my home wherever I go."
"Harvesting in autumn and garnering in winter."
"One word out of the mouth and even a team of four horses cannot overtake it."
"A rootless plant at the top of the mountain; no wind is blowing, but see how the leaves sway."

"Even a fist angrily lifted would not strike the smiling baby."
"This body from head to toe is not worth five cents."
"The body is lying on the vast expanse of waves; see the man carrying a torch in the broad daylight."
"A dish of gruel in the morning and rice for noon."
"There is in the kitchen no extra meal for a visitor."
"The cock made of mud, the dog made of brick."
"However lovingly cherished flowers soon wither away; however despised and down-trodden weeds never cease to grow."
"The sleeves being too short, the arms are bare."
"Tumbling over again and again."
"The three-legged toad carries an enormous elephant on its back."

The above quotations are enough to show where is the abode of the Zen master, that is, in what "household air" he is living. However enigmatically these passages may appear, their fundamental keynote is what is technically called "deeds of no purpose" or "a life of effortlessness," or in Sanskrit anabhogacaryā.

All the Mahayana Sūtras give the greatest significance to the attainment of this "life of no-purposiveness." The lilies of the field are living it, so are all the greatest spiritual leaders of the world. And all the "Great Vows" of the Bodhisattva grow out of it; his vows are no vows in the ordinary sense of the word.

Among the few incidents in connection with the Zendo life we must not forget mentioning are the tea-ceremony which takes place twice a month on the first and on the fifteenth, a sort of examination which takes place at the end of a term, and the bell, the ringing of which is so expressive of the spirit of Buddhism which is found moving in the depths of its followers and also of Oriental people generally.

The tea-ceremony is a simple affair but the fact that all the monks together with the Rōshi partake of the tea from one teapot is indicative of the democratic and brotherly feeling which is at the bottom of the Zendo life. Sometimes the Rōshi may give them a little talk about the study of Zen or the doings of the ancient masters and shake them up to new redoubled efforts. Simplicity and orderliness is the one prevailing and most noticeable spirit in all the aspects of Zendo life, but there is no military austerity here (Plate 41).

At the end of each sojourn, the summer and the winter, each monk is taken to task to render account for his behaviour during the term. He is then free to leave the monastery where he has spent his term and go somewhere else. Each is summoned before the chief monk-official and asked what he is going to do now that the angya season has set in and he is at liberty to take advantage of it. If he expresses the desire to leave for one reason or another, he is so registered in the book. But if he wishes to continue his Zendo life here, the chief monk may have something to say about his conduct during the period that has just past. If the monk behaved properly, he will pass without much comment. When otherwise, he will quite severely be reprimanded for his misdemeanour, and in some extreme cases even a refusal to renew his term will be the verdict. This is fatal to the career of the

TEA-CEREMONY WITH ROSHI PLATE 41

monk, because the stain clings to him wherever he goes, and all the Zendo doors may be found closed to him. This term-end examination is therefore quite a nerve-racking event in the life of the Zendo monk (Plate 42).

There are several kinds of bell[4] used in the monastery for different purposes; the one shown here in the picture is the largest (Plate 43). It rings regularly at least four or five times a day; in the morning it reports the time for the monks to wake up, which is about half past three, and in the evening to start their evening meditation, and at night to keep up their exercise in a reclining position, which is about nine or half past nine.

The spirit of Buddhism is most intimately connected with the big bell, apart from which we cannot think of the monastery life. The meaning of the bell is revealed in a most significant way: when the dusk approaches, the clouds grow chillier, the air is perfectly still, the pale and almost indistinguishable new moon is about to set, and the birds quite tired after a day's labour seek their nests for the night among the mountain trees, then the bell begins to ring its evening mission. As the solid body of metal hollowed out is struck with a heavy piece of wood, a soft, resonant, soul-pacifying sound issues from it, which fills and reverberates through the entire valley. If we are near enough, we shall hear the monk recite the Kwannon-gyō—a fitting accompaniment to the booming bell.

Yün-mên (Ummon) once had a bell made; when it reached his monastery, the monks asked the master to strike it to celebrate the occasion. He gave it the first stroke, and the monks followed him. The master asked: "What do you want to do by striking the bell?" The monks: "To invite the master to a feast." Yün-mên was not satisfied with the answer and gave his own: "To stop suffering, to put an end to sorrow."

On another occasion, seeing a monk strike the bell, Yün-mên asked: "Who made this bell?" The monk gave no answer, where-

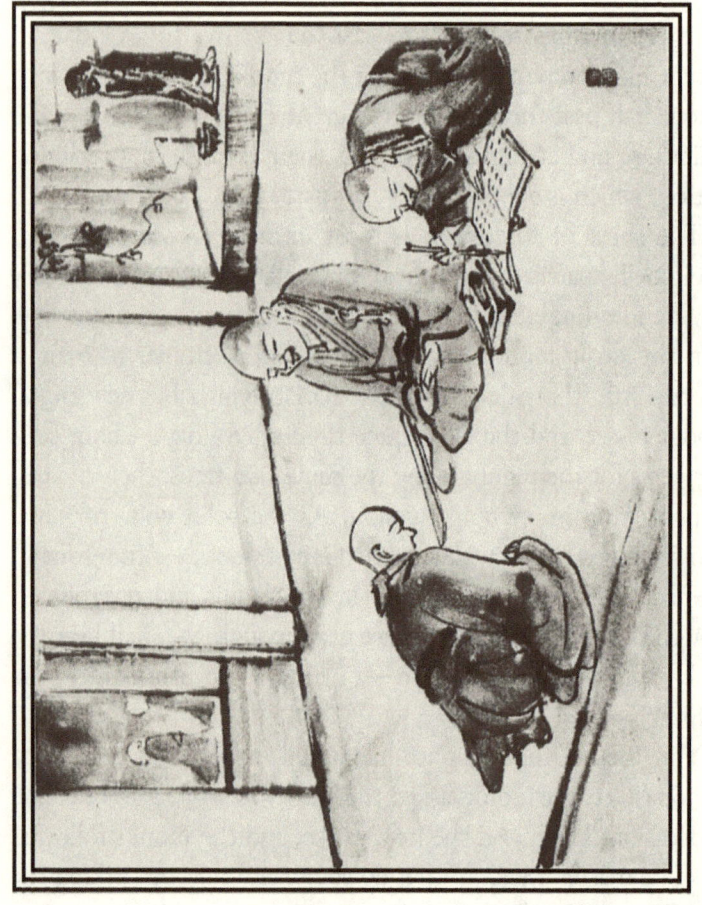

TERM-END EXAMINATION PLATE 42

upon the master said: "You ask me and I will give you an answer." The monk asked, and the master said: "The monks." Another response given by the master was that he struck the bell once by himself saying "Mahā-prajña-pāramitā!" Yün-men once announced that "True emptiness does not destroy existence as it is (astitva); true emptiness does not differ from form (rūpam)." The monk asked: "What is true emptiness?" The master said, "Do you hear the bell?" The monk answered: "That is the sound of the bell." Yün-mên concluded, "You wouldn't understand even when you wait for an ass year to come."[5]

The following poem on the bell was composed by Sōyen Shaku (died 1919), of Kamakura :

"In early morning it wakes one from a long night's slumber, enveloped in clouds of ignorance;
At close of day it makes one turn towards the perfect moon of Truth, shining in the sky of vast emptiness;
Where there is nothing heard, nothing taught, nothing done and doing,
The booming bell goes on filling the air and shaking up the entire Brahma heaven."

The following is by Ju-ching on a little hanging bell under the eaves; he was the teacher of Dōgen while the latter was studying Zen in China between 1223-1228:

"The whole body is the mouth, hanging in the air;
It is unconcerned which way the wind blows; East or West, North or South;
Without distinction it gives out its own sermon on the Prajñā: *Ti ting tung, ti ting tung,* and again *ti ting tung.*"

Footnotes

1 The illustrations of the various sound instruments used in the Zen monastery are given below.

2. The following is the Case I of the Hekigan, omitting all the commentary insertions by Yengo and also his general remarks on the Case I as well as on Seccho's verse.

3. Literally: one may rise in the east and sink in the west; one may walk against or in accord with; one may go straight ahead or crosswise; whether to give up or to take away from, one is in perfect freedom.

4. See the Appendix.

5. The ass is not found among the twelve animals figuring in the Chinese calendar.

APPENDICES & GLOSSARY

The Name of the Ten Buddhas

1. Vairocana Buddha as the Dharmakāya, Pure and Undefiled;
2. Locana Buddha¹ as the Sambhogakāya, Perfect and Full;
3. Śākyamuni Buddha as the Nirmanakaya, Whose Forms are Manifested in Hundreds of Thousands of Katis;
4. Maitreya the Venerable Buddha, Who is to be Born Here in Time to Come;
5. All the Buddhas of the Past, Present, and Future in All the Ten Quarters;
6. Mañjuśrī the Bodhisattva of Great Wisdom;
7. Samantabhadra the Bodhisattva of Great Deeds;
8. Avalokiteśvara the Bodhisattva of Great Love;
9. All the Venerable Bodhisattva-Mahāsattvas;
10. Mahāprajñapāramitā².

Verse of the Morning Gruel Meal

The gruel-meal has ten advantages
Whereby the Yogins are benefitted;
The results accruing from it are boundless,
Finally leading them to eternal happiness.

D.T. SUZUKI

Verse after the Morning Gruel-Meal

Having finished the morning gruel-meal,
Let us pray that all beings
Accomplish whatever task they are engaged in
And be furnished with all the Buddha-dharmas.

Verse of the Midday Meal

The meal has three virtues and six tastes,
Offered to the Buddha and the Brotherhood;
Let all sentient beings in the Dharmadhatu,
Universally share alike the offering.

Verse of the Saba

O you of the spiritual worlds,
I now offer this to you;
Let this food fill the ten quarters
And all the spirits enjoy it.

The Five Reflections

First, let us reflect on our own work, let us see whence this comes;
Secondly, let us reflect how imperfect our virtue is, whether we deserve this offering;
Thirdly, What is most essential is to hold our minds in control and be detached from the various faults, greed, etc.
Fourthly, That this is taken as medicinal is to keep our bodies in good health;
Fifthly, In order to accomplish the task of enlightenment, we accept this food.

Verse of the Three Morsels of Food

The first morsel is to destroy all evils,
The second morsel is to practise all good deeds,
The third morsel is to save all sentient beings
May we all attain the path of Buddhahood.

Verse of the Waste Water

This water wherewith the bowls were cleansed,
Has the taste of heavenly nectar;
I offer it to you hosts of the spiritual realms,
May you all be filled and satisfied! Om, Ma-ku-la-sai Svaha!

Verse After the Midday Meal

Having finished the rice-meal, my bodily strength is fully restored,
My power extends over the ten quarters and through the three periods of time, and I am a strong man;
As to reversing the wheel of cause and effect, no thought is to be wasted over it;
May all beings attain miraculous powers!

The Mirror of Advice

The most important thing to do for the Zen monks of our school is to understand the koans left by the ancient masters. There are recently, however, some ill-advised fellows who are quite ignorant of the meaning of the thoughtful contrivance bequeathed by wise men of the past; they despise the ancient wisdom, not allowing [their pupils] to study it with due care. Our own monk-students, failing to weigh properly the merit of such a misguided attitude of those ignorant critics, bury themselves in the den of the ghostly beings; they make light of the ancient koans and are vainly proud of this fact before well-seasoned followers of Zen. They are truly to be pitied, and also to be laughed at.

Those who come to study Zen under my guidance should cherish a grave doubt, each according to his capacities, as to the meaning of the ancient koans as if his head were set on fire. Let them keep on, without interruption, doubting the koans until they come to realise a state of great fixation. When this state of fixation is broken through, they are able to leap out of the cave of birth and death. Then they can penetratingly understand what was in the hearts of the wise men of old. This is the time when they feel at ease with themselves and are able to requite all the kindly feelings the Buddhas and Fathers have cherished for them. Why then should they waste this precious life of theirs by not doing anything serious or of enough importance?

RULES REGULATING THE DAILY LIFE[3]

The most urgent task is to study and master Zen. Therefore, whenever you have a view to discuss with the master, consult with the directing monk (jikijitsu) and try to see the master regardless of the hours of the day.

1. When entering the Zendo, fold your hands, palm to palm, before your chest; when going out of it, hold your hands, the right over the left, in front of the chest. Let your walking and standing be duly decorous. Do not walk across the front of the Mañjuśrī shrine; be not in a flurry or swaggering when walking the floor.

2. During the meditation hours, no one is permitted to leave the Hall except for interviewing the master. To other necessary movements, the intermission hours are to be devoted. While outside, no whispering, no tarrying is allowed.

3. When the kinhin (walking) goes on, do not remain in your seats; when walking do not shuffle your sandals. If you are, on account of disease, prevented from taking part in the kinhin, with the consent of the directing monk (jikijitsu) stand on the floor at your seat.

4. The keisaku (warning-stick) is to be used with discrimination on the monks, whether they are dozing or not. When submitting to the warning stick, courteously fold your hands and bow; do not permit any egoistic thoughts to assert themselves and cherish anger.

5. At the time of tea-ceremony (sarei) taking place twice a day, no one shall be absent; no left-overs are to be thrown on the floor.

6. No sundry articles are to be scattered about your seats (tan). No writing materials are allowed. Do not take off your upper garment at your seats when going out of the back door.

7. Even when the Zendo is not in regular session, you are not to pass your time dozing, sitting against the back-wall.

8. No one is allowed on his own accord to use the warning-stick (keisaku) although he may be suffering from the stiffness of his shoulder-muscles.

9. Going out to town or visiting the Jōjū quarters is not permitted: if absolutely necessary, transact the business through the attendants (jisha) of the Zendo; otherwise, all private affairs are to be settled on the "needle and moxa" days (hashin kyūji).

10. On ordinary days the monks are not allowed at the attendants' quarters (jisharyo); if necessary, the jikijitsu (directing monk) is to be notified.

11. At the time of morning service, the dozing ones are to be severely dealt with the keisaku (warning-stick).

12. At meal-time the monks are to conduct themselves quietly and to make no noise in the handling of the bowls; the waiting monks should move about quietly and in due decorum.

13. When the meditation hours are over at night, go right to bed; do not disturb others by sutra-reading, or bowings, or whispering with the neighbouring monks.

14. During the term, the monks are not allowed to leave

the monastery unless their teachers or parents are critically ill or dead.

15. When a monk is newly admitted into the Brotherhood, the fact is announced and he takes the seat assigned to him; but before this is done, he must first make bows to the Holy Monk (i.e., Mañjusrī), And then pay his respect to the head of the tan and to the jikijitsu (directing monk).

16. When the monks go out for their begging round, they are not to swing their arms, or put their hands inside the dress, or walk the streets staggeringly, or whisper to one another; for such behaviours are damaging to the dignity of monkhood. If they meet horses, carriages, etc., in the streets, be careful to avoid walking against them. In all their movements, the monks ought to be orderly.

17. The days bearing the numbers four and nine, are the days for general sweeping, shaving, bathing, working outdoors, etc.; sewing, moxa-burning, etc. may also take place on these days. The monks are then not supposed to visit one another and pass their time in talking idly, cracking jokes, and laughing nonsensically.

18. As to fixing bath days for the Brotherhood, the monks entrusted with the task are requested to consult the shikaryo (head of the general office) and act according to his directions.

19. When any one is indisposed, the matter is to be reported to the jikijitsu and the attendant-monk (jisha), and the sick one will be removed from the Zendo. While being nursed, he is neither to read books, nor to be engaged in literary work, nor to pass his time in idle talk. If he comes back after five days, he is expected to perform the rite of "returning to the Zendo."

The above regulations are to be carefully taken notice of. Those who violate belong to the family of the Evil One and interfere with the welfare of the community. They are to be expelled speedily after holding a council. The reason is to preserve as long as possible the life of the community.

REGULATIONS OF THE SICK-ROOM

Anyone who happens to be the occupant of this room because of ill health, is not to forget practising zazen silently along with taking medicine, even with his head on the pillow. Never neglect exercising himself in the cultivation of the right thought. When this is not done, the disease may be aggravated and the medicine cease to be effective. Three doses of medicine are to be taken daily; each basketful of charcoal costs three sen.[4]

1. Fire of all kind is to be carefully kept under control.
2. Neither sake nor herbs of the onion family are allowed even as medicine. According to the nature of the disease, special cooking is allowed after reporting to the office. Other things are prohibited.
3. Be careful not to soil the bedding, etc.
4. While in sick-bed, a monk is not allowed to read books, to engage in literary work, or to idle away his time in trivial talk. If he comes out of the sick-room after staying away for five days, he is expected to perform the rite of "returning to the Zendo."

REGULATIONS OF THE OFFICIAL QUARTERS (JYŌJŪ)⁵

The most essential business of monkhood is to study Zen, and you are expected to exert yourselves in this. After the daily work, keep your evening meditation as in the Zendo. Says an ancient master, "The exercise while working is hundreds of thousands of times more valuable than the one practised while in quietude." Keeping this in mind, exert yourselves to the best of your abilities.

1. Take the best care of all kinds of fire and light.

2. At the morning and the evening service and on other occasions requiring attendance, the monk-officials are not to fall behind the others.

3. At meal-times try by all means to attend a second sitting if you are detained by your work. In handling the bowls, in sipping soup, you are not to make a noise. The waiting-monks must behave orderly and with decorum.

4. In going the begging rounds or in performing outdoor work, you are also expected to join the others; if you are prevented from this, do not neglect reporting the fact at the shikaryo.

5. Do not visit other official rooms and spend the time in gossipping and talking trivialities whereby interrupting their hours of meditation. When business requires visits, do not prolong them beyond absolute necessity.

6. Going out in town is strictly forbidden. If it is necessary to go out of the gate, the shikaryo is to be notified. When out in town the mannerly behaviour of monkhood is expected.

7. When sick and not able to attend the service, etc., the fact is to be reported at the shikaryo; such monks are not to

visit other official rooms.

8. When the evening meditation hours are over, each monk is to retire at once to his own bed. No wastage of the light is allowed by sitting up late and talking nonsense. The bedding and other articles are to be kept clean.

9. All the articles and pieces of furniture belonging to the Jyōjū quarters are to be used with the utmost care. After use, take note to return them where they are kept. Says an ancient master: "All the belongings of the Jyōjū are to be used as a man does his own eyes."

10. The sandals are not to be left carelessly on the floor. While stepping up and down the hall, do not make rustling sounds. Do not make light of the trivial deeds of daily life, for great virtues are born of them. Pray, be mindful of all that has been stated above.

REGULATIONS OF THE LODGING ROOM

Monks intently bent on the mastery of Zen go on a pilgrimage in search of an able master and superior friends. When the evening comes, they find out a monastery where they may pass the night. Being permitted to the lodging room, they release themselves of the travelling outfit, and sit in the meditation posture facing the wall. It is to be most regretted that recently there are some travelling monks who have no desire to conduct themselves in accordance with old usage. The main point for the monks, however, is to devote their entire energy to the settlement of the gravest business they can have in this life in whatever surroundings they may find themselves. The meaning of the pilgrimage in Zen lies nowhere else but here, as was anciently seen in the company of Seppo, Ganto, and Kinzan. O monks, be ever diligent!

1. After the evening bell is struck, no travelling monks are admitted.

2. Do not ask for a second night's lodging however stormy and windy the day may be. In case of sickness this rule is waved.

3. No dozing against the travelling bag is allowed. The lodging monk is not to go to bed until the evening meditation hours are over or until a notice to that effect is given to him.

4. Attend the morning service when the bell in the Hall is heard; the kesa may be omitted.

5. The morning gruel is served when the umpan ("cloud-board") is struck.

6. No light is to be burned in the night.

EGULATIONS OF THE BATH-ROOM

While taking a bath, the "exquisite touch" of warmth must be made to lead to the "realisation of the nature of water."[6] No idle talking is allowed here. Before and after the bath, proper respect is to be paid to the venerable Bhadra.

1. The best care must be taken of fire.

2. The bath-room work is attended in turn by the monks from the Zendo. Otherwise, orders are issued from the shikaryo.

3. When the master takes his bath, have his attendants notified. In case of other respectable personages, special attention will be given to the cleanliness and orderliness of the bath-room.

4. When the bath is ready, the wooden blocks are clapped

according to the regulations, and the monks led in rotation to the room by the Zendo attendants.

5. For the fuel, dead leaves gathered from the woods and other waste materials are to be used.

6. When the bathing is all over, be thorough in scraping all the embers and hot ashes out from under the bathing pot and have them completely extinguished.

7. On the day following, the bath-tub will be thoroughly scrubbed, and the entire room nicely cleansed, while the vessels are properly arranged.

The above articles are to be observed at all points. No random use of the bath-room is permitted, which may interrupt the speedy execution of the public office.

THE SOUND INSTRUMENTS IN THE ZEN MONASTERY

In the Zendo life, the movements of the monks on various occasions are directed by the use of different kinds of sound producing instruments. No oral orders are given; but when a certain instrument is sounded, the monks know what it means at that particular time. The accompanying pictures[7] illustrate such instruments.

The ōgane (1)[8] is the largest bell used in the monastery, It hangs underneath a specially-designed structure as illustrated in Plate 43. The heavy swinging beam (2, shumoku) is used to strike the bell. It is this bell which reflects the spirit of the Buddhist temple. The ring has a peculiarly soul-pacifying effect. Lafcadio Hearn in his Unfamiliar Japan, Vol. I refers to the "big bell of Engakuji" and most beautifully describes its

THE SECRET WORLD OF THE ZEN BUDDHIST MONK

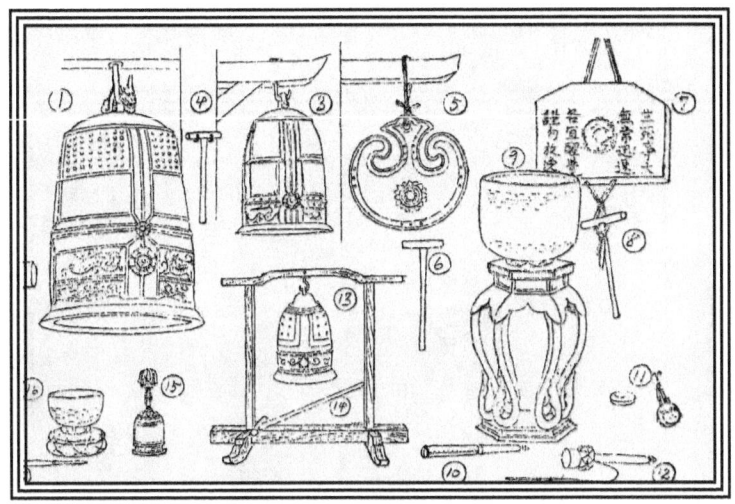

SOUND INSTRUMENTS I

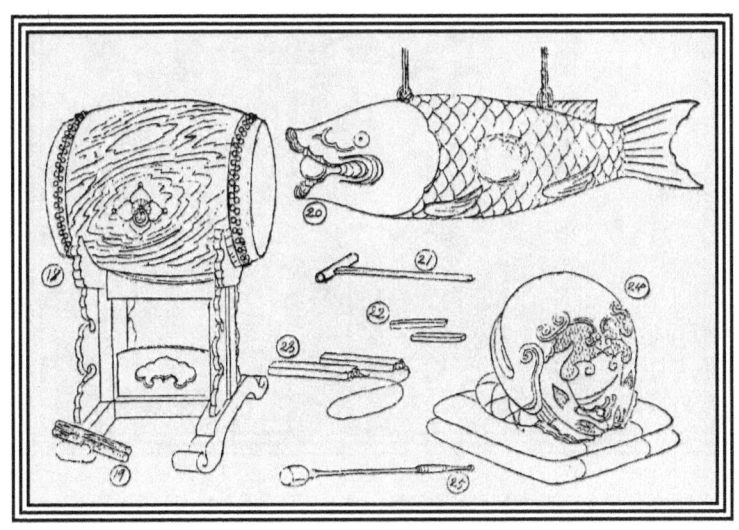

SOUND INSTRUMENTS II

MONKS STRIKING THE LARGE BELL PLATE 43

"sweet billowing of tone" when it is struck and the "eddying of waves of echoes" which rolls over the surrounding hills. As a work of art the bell occupies an important position, and there are many old bells now in Japan which are classed as "national treasures" of the country.[9]

Denshō or Hanshō (3) is a much smaller one and generally found hanging under the eaves. It is struck with a mallet (4). When a gathering takes place in the Buddha-hall, this calls out the monks from the Zendo.

Umpan (5) is "cloud-plate" made of bronze. When this rings, it means that the dining room is open.

Han (7) is a heavy solid board of wood hung by the front door of the Zendo. When this is struck, the monks know that the time is come for them to get up or to retire to bed or that a teishō is to take place, etc. The characters read:

"Birth-and-death is the grave event,
Transiency will soon be here,
Let each wake up [to this fact],
And, being ever reverend, do not give yourselves up to dissipation."

The last two lines sometimes read differently in different Zendos. The board is taken hold of, when struck, by means of the strings hanging below in a loop.

Kin or Keisu (9) is a high, somewhat large, metal gong in the Buddha-hall. Its rim is struck with a stick (10) to punctuate the sutra-reading. The smaller one, Bin or Shōkei (16), is also used in this connection.

Two kinds of bells (suzu or rei) used by Rōshi are shown in (11). The choice is individual. Other kinds are also used, one of which is given in (15).

Inkin (12) is always carried in the hand and struck with a metal stick attached to it with a string. When the head-monk strikes it in the Zendo, it means the beginning or the end of the meditation hours. When he does so at the head of a procession it means that all the monks joining it are to stand still and then sit, or that they have to rise from the sitting position and walk back to the Zendo.

Kanshō (13) is used when the monks want to interview the Rōshi on Zen. When the sanzen hour comes, the Rōshi's attendant strikes this bell with the hammer (14). The monks come out of the Zendo, one by one if it is a dokusan, and in file if it is a sōsan; they sit before the bell in the order of arrival. The master interviews one monk at a time. Being ready, he rings his hand-bell (11) to which the monk responds by striking his bell (13), once for sōsan and twice for dokusan.

Rei (15), also called Bin, is a hand-bell which rings by shaking. It is used by Rōshi, and also by a monk when he reads the Sūtras while standing, for instance, before Idaten, the kitchen god, at meal time.

The big drum, Hokku (18), is generally set up on a high stand in a corner of the Buddha-hall. When a general gathering takes place, it is beaten with two sticks (19) alternately with a peculiar rhythm.

The big wooden fish (20) called Ho is used principally in the Soto monastery and not in the Rinzai. The inside is hollowed out. It is used to announce the midday meal. How the fish came to function in the Buddhist temple is unknown. Some think the fish is a symbol of immortality, and for this reason it is frequently found in Christian symbolism. But

Buddhism is the teaching in which rebirth and not individual immortality is emphasised.

Mokugyo (24), literally "a wooden fish" is said to be the modification of the Ho (20). It is a peculiarly-shaped roundish solid block of wood with the inside hollowed out, and obtainable in all sizes, the smallest being as small as one inch on its longer side while the larger ones may measure even more than three feet. It has a fish-scale pattern on its body and where it tapers off into the form of a handle, a pair of eyes is carved. It is beaten with a stick, the top part of which is stuffed and wrapped with leather (25). The sound thus emitted has a strange hypnotic effect on the hearer. When it accompanies the sutra-reading, for example, before a teishō, it makes the minds of the audience properly receptive for what is to come.

There are two kinds of clappers, Hyōshigi (22 and 23) in use in the monastery. They are solid pieces of hard wood: the larger ones may be somewhat longer than one foot in length and the smaller ones about half a foot. The latter are used in the Zendo while the former are used outside, for instance, when the monks are about to eat, when the bath is ready, and on other occasions.

Footnotes

1. Notice the distinction made between Vairocana Buddha and Locana Buddha, while practically they are the same.
2. The presence of Mahāprajñapāramitā in the list of the ten Buddhas is significant. In fact, whenever prayers are offered, "Mahāprajñapāramitā" is always mentioned together with "all the Buddhas and Venerable Bodhisattva mahāsattvas" as if it were something quite personal.

D.T. SUZUKI

3. This applies to the Dōnai, i.e., Zendo proper where the monks observe the meditation hours. As to the distinction between Dōnai and Jyōju, see below, where the Jyōju regulations are given.

4. These regulations were compiled many years ago before prices began to go up after the Great War.

5. Literally meaning "eternally abiding." The monastery where Zen is studied is divided into two sections: jyōju and dōnai. The Jyōjii section is the official or business quarters where affairs connected with the Zendo life are carried out, such as cooking meals for the monks, taking care of the Buddha-hall, planning for daily work, getting provisions, seeing visitors, paying bills, receiving donations, etc. For these offices, elder monks of some experience are chosen, and change of personnel takes place every few months. They have their own separate rooms outside the Zendo. The dōnai means "within the Zendo, or Soda." This is where the monks generally have their seats of meditation.

6. See the seventy-eighth case of the Hekigan (*Pi-yen-chi*). Cf. p.61, of the present work.

7 See p.155.

8. The figures in parentheses refer to the illustrations on p.155.

9. Sōyen Shaku's poem on p.139 of this book refers to this *Ogane*, while Ju-ching's is what is known as wind-bell (fêng-ling).

Glossary of the Japanese Terms

Angya, "going on foot," Zen pilgrimage.
Densuryō, office in charge of the Buddha Hall.
Dokusan, individual *sanzen* voluntarily done.
Dōnai, another name for Zendo, as distinguished from the office quarters called.
Enjudō, "life-prolonging room," where the sick are taken care of.
Fūsuryō, office where all accounts regarding the Zendo life are kept.
Futon, quilt filled with cotton-wool.
Geta, foot-gear made of wood.
Hashin kyūji, "taking-up needles and treating with moxa."
Higan, "the other side," *pāramitā*; the *higan* season is March 18-24 and September 21-27, when people visit the temples and decorate the graves.
Hōjō, "ten feet square," abbot's quarters.
Inryō, "retreat-room" for Rōshi (master of the Zendo).
Jikijitsu, head-monk and director of the Zendo.
Jisha, attendant.
Jisharyō, attendants' office attached to the Zendo.
Jōju, official quarters, where the business side of the Zendo life is carried on.
Kafū, "household air."
Keisaku, warning staff.
Kesa, *kaṣāya* in Sanskrit, the official or ceremonial dress worn by Buddhist priests and monks.
Kesa-bunko, a box in which *kesa* is kept and carried.
Kinhin, walking exercise in the Zendo.
Koan, to be pronounced ko-an; a problem given by the master for solution.
Kōza, discourse on a Zen textbook.

Kwatz!, an ejaculation given by the Zen masters, especially connected with Rinzai, originator of the Rinzai school of Zen Buddhism.

Kyōgai, *gocara* in Sanskrit, general mental attitude, the basic tone of one's inner life.

Mokugyo, a wooden sound-producing implement used in accompaniment with the sutra-reading.

Niwa-dzume, "occupying the court," one of the experiences a novice-monk has to go through before his admittance into the monastery.

Otoki, dinner.

Rōshi, master, "old teacher."

Saiza, dinner

Sake, intoxicant made from rice.

Sanzen, studying Zen.

Sarei, tea-drinking ceremony.

Satori, understanding the truth of Zen.

Segaki, feeding the hungry ghosts; gaki=preta in Sanskrit.

Semmon Dōjō, Zen institute.

Sesshin, a special period devoted to the study of Zen.

Shikaryo, originally, office entertaining visitors, but nowadays in combination with Fusūryō, a general directing office.

Tan, raised tatami floor in the Zendo.

Tangwa-dzume, "occupying the lodging room," where the novice monk has to stay for a few days before he is admitted into the Zendo.

Tan-to, head of the *tan*.

Tatami, a straw matting about 3x6 feet.

Teisho, same as kōza, Rōshi's talk on a Zen textbook.

Tendoku, "reading by revolving."

Tenzoryo, office in charge of provisions and cooking.

Umpan, bronze board with cloud-design, used to call monks to meal.

Yakuseki, evening meal taken as a "medicine."

Zagu, a piece of cloth carried by the Zen monk on which his bowing is done.
Zazen, sitting in Zen meditation.
Zempanryo, quarters reserved for Rōshi.
Zendo, the building where monks live apart from the Jōjū quarters.

About D.T. Suzuki

Daisetsz Teitaro Suzuki (1870–1966) was a student of the Zen master Shaku Soen and a Japanese author of books and essays on Buddhism, Zen and Shin that were instrumental in spreading interest in Far Eastern philosophy to the West. Suzuki was also a prolific translator of Chinese, Japanese, and Sanskrit literature. He spent several lengthy stretches teaching or lecturing at Western universities, and devoted many years to a professorship at Ōtani University, a Japanese Buddhist school.

Morgan Buchanan has taught Taoist philosophy, meditation and tai chi for over twenty years in both the United States and Australia. He is a published author, has lectured at universities, appeared on national radio and is a regular guest speaker at interfaith conferences. He is a student of Master Law Lun Yeung. For three years he was part of an interfaith household with Rev. Dr. John Dupuche, Lama Lobsang Tendar and Swami Sanyasanand.

ABOUT FLOATING WORLD PRESS

Japanese woodblock prints from the Edo period are termed *ukiyo-e* — images of the floating world. The term ukiyo is also an ironic allusion to the homophone *ukiyo* ("Sorrowful World"), the earthly plane of death and rebirth from which Buddhists sought release. Floating World press is dedicated to publishing unusual, interesting and enlightening books that promote a cultural harmony between East and West. Our books seek to embody a traditional aesthetic of form and function — beautiful words, beautiful design. For more information visit us at

www.floatingworldpress.com

www.ingramcontent.com/pod-product-compliance
Lightning Source LLC
Chambersburg PA
CBHW020356170426

43200CB00005B/191